G.I. GURDJIEFF
The War Against Sleep

G.I. GURDJIEFF

by

Colin Wilson

THE AQUARIAN PRESS

First published 1980
This edition, revised and expanded, 1986

ESSEX COUNTY LIBRARY

British Library Cataloguing in Publication Data

Wilson, Colin, *1931-*
G. I. Gurdjieff: the war against sleep.—Rev.
and expanded.
1. Gurdjieff, George
I. Title   II. Wilson, Colin, *1931*—War against
sleep
197.2   B4249.G84

ISBN 0-85030-503-9

*The Aquarian Press is part of the Thorsons Publishing Group,
Wellingborough, Northamptonshire, NN8 2RQ, England*

Printed in Great Britain by Woolnough Bookbinding Limited,
Irthlingborough, Northamptonshire

3 5 7 9 10 8 6 4

For
Cyril Tilburn, whose help was invaluable.

Contents

Acknowledgements

I wish to acknowledge the kindness of Messrs Routledge and Kegan Paul for permission to quote from the works of Gurdjieff and Ouspensky. I also wish to thank Turnstone Press Ltd. for allowing me to quote from John Bennett's *Witness* and *Gurdjieff: Making a New World*. I also wish to thank Victor Gollancz Ltd. for permission to quote from Fritz Peters's *Boyhood with Gurdjieff*.

Introductory Note

IT WAS in 1951, a year after the publication of *In Search of the Miraculous* and *Beelzebub's Tales to His Grandson,* that I first came across the ideas of Gurdjieff. I was instantly aware of being in touch with one of the great minds of this century. I wrote about him for the first time in 1955, in the concluding chapter of *The Outsider,* where he figures (with Ramakrishna and T. E. Hulme) as one of the few men who have glimpsed a solution to the 'sickness of man in the twentieth century'. Since then I have written about him in several books – notably *The Occult* and *Mysteries.*

When the publishers of the present book suggested that I should write about Gurdjieff, I experienced misgivings; it would involve repeating a great deal that I have already written. But then, my own views on Gurdjieff have changed and evolved over the years, and the idea of getting them between two covers was an interesting challenge. So I brushed aside my doubts, decided to repeat myself where necessary, and wrote the book. And in repeating myself I discovered an entirely new set of meanings and implications in Gurdjieff.

It was an interesting lesson in the difference between 'grasping' and merely 'knowing' – a distinction that lies at the heart of Gurdjieff's thought.

Which is why I make no apology to those who have read me on Gurdjieff before. His ideas will bear repetition.

One

The Magician

ON A BRIGHT summer morning in 1917, an attractive Russian woman in her late twenties sat in Phillipov's café, in St Petersburg's Nevsky Prospect, waiting for the arrival of her friend Peter Demianovitch Ouspensky. Uncharacteristically, Ouspensky was late. When he finally hurried in, he was in a state of unusual excitement. His first words were: 'I think this time we've really found what we need.' And he reminded her that in Moscow, in 1915, he had met a remarkable teacher, who spoke of the fundamental problems of human existence with an air of knowledge and authority. His name was George Ivanovitch Gurdjieff. Now, said Ouspensky, Gurdjieff had come to St Petersburg – and was, at that very moment, waiting for them in another branch of Phillipov's across the road. The lady, Anna Butkovsky, says:

When I entered the other Phillipov's I saw a man sitting at a table in the far corner, wearing an ordinary black coat and the high astrakhan cap that Russian men wear in winter. Signs of Greek ancestry could be discerned in his fine, virile features and in the look that pierced right through you (though not in an unpleasant way). He had an oval-shaped head, black eyes and an olive complexion, and wore a black moustache. His manner was very calm and relaxed, and he spoke without any gesticulation. Even to be sitting with him was very agreeable. Though it was not his native language, he could speak Russian fluently, in a manner not quite like ours, more exact and very picturesque. Sometimes he would speak in a 'lazy' voice, and you felt that each phrase was being carefully and specially put together, for that particular occasion, not at all like the ready-made phrases which we would normally use in conversation, devoid of creative power or individuality. You quickly grasped that he had a gift of assembling words expressively. And here I sat, and I felt that I was at last in the presence of a Guru.

Gurdjieff made the same kind of impression on everyone who met him. We have, perhaps, a dozen records by pupils describing their first meeting. Almost without exception, they mention that 'look that pierced right through you'. A young army officer named Thomas de Hartmann met Gurdjieff at about the same time. When two men wearing black coats and black moustaches approached him in the café, he wondered which was Gurdjieff. 'But my uncertainty was quickly dispelled by the eyes of one of the men'. J. G. Bennett, who met Gurdjieff in Constantinople in 1920, wrote: 'I met the strangest pair of eyes I have ever seen. The two eyes were so different that I wondered if the light had played some trick on me.' And all these different impressions are summarized in a remark made by the wife of the physician Kenneth Walker after she met Gurdjieff in Paris in 1948: 'The chief impression he gave me was the impression of immense vigour and of concentrated strength. I had the feeling that he was not really a man but a magician.'

Gurdjieff was, in fact, a kind of magician. There can be no doubt that he possessed certain magical or psychic powers. But he seems to have regarded these as irrelevant or unimportant. Gurdjieff's central concern was with the *potentialities* of human beings – or, more specifically, of human consciousness. Ouspensky expressed it clearly in a little book called *The Psychology of Man's Possible Evolution*, where he remarks that ordinary psychology is concerned with man as he actually exists. But there is another kind, that studies man 'not from the point of view of what he is, or what he seems to be, but from the point of view of what he may become; that is, from the point of view of his possible evolution.'

Expressed in this way, the idea sounds vague and general. But Gurdjieff's approach was precise and particular. The writings of his pupils – or disciples – contains many accounts of the operation of his own remarkable powers. Fritz Peters, an American who had known Gurdjieff since childhood, describes what happened when he visited Gurdjieff in Paris immediately after the Second World War. His war experiences had brought Peters to the verge of a nervous breakdown. The moment Gurdjieff saw him, he realized that he was sick.

When we reached his apartment, he led me down a long hall to a dark bedroom, indicated the bed, told me to lie down, and said: 'This is your room, for as long as you need it.' I laid down on the bed and he left the room but did not close the door. I felt such enormous relief and such excitement at seeing him that I began to cry uncontrollably and then my head began to pound. I could not rest and got up and walked to the kitchen where I found him sitting at the table. He looked alarmed when he saw me, and asked me what was wrong. I said I needed some aspirin or something for my headache, but he shook his head, stood up, and pointed to the other chair by the kitchen table. 'No medicine,' he said firmly. 'I give you coffee. Drink as hot as you can.' I sat at the table while he heated the coffee and then served it to me. He then walked across the small room to stand in front of the refrigerator and watch me. I could not take my eyes off him and realized that he looked incredibly weary – I have never seen anyone look so tired. I remembered being slumped over the table, sipping at my coffee, when I began to feel a strange uprising of energy within myself – I stared at him, automatically straightened up, and it was as if a violent electric blue light emanated from him and entered into me. As this happened, I could feel the tiredness drain out of me, but at the same moment his body slumped and his face turned grey as if it was being drained of life. I looked at him, amazed, and when he saw me sitting erect, smiling and full of energy, he said quickly: 'You all right now – watch food on stove – I must go.' There was something very urgent in his voice and I leaped to my feet to help him but he waved me away and limped slowly out of the room.

What had happened, apparently, was that Gurdjieff had somehow *poured* vital energy into Peters by some psychic discipline – either that, or somehow touched the source of vitality in Peters himself; at all events, it drained Gurdjieff. Peters says: 'I was convinced ... that he knew how to transmit energy from himself to others; I was also convinced that it could only be done at great cost to himself.'

What happened next is equally significant.

It also became obvious within the next few minutes that he

knew how to renew his own energy quickly, for I was amazed when he returned to the kitchen to see the change in him; he looked like a young man again, alert, smiling, sly and full of good spirits. He said that this was a very fortunate meeting, and that while I had forced him to make an almost impossible effort, it had been – as I had witnessed – a very good thing for both of us.

Gurdjieff's comment is of considerable importance. When Peters first came to the apartment, he looked tired – 'I have never seen anyone look so tired.' He made an effort that drained him even further, transmitting vitality to Peters. And then, within fifteen minutes, was completely renewed and refreshed. The implication seems clear. Gurdjieff himself had *forgotten* that he had the power to renew his own energies, until the exhaustion of Fritz Peters forced him to make an enormous effort. Before Peters came, Gurdjieff had been taking his own fatigue for granted, as something inevitable. Pouring energy into Peters reminded him that he had the power to somehow call upon vital energy. This is why he told Peters that this was a fortunate meeting for both of them.

This story enables us to see precisely why Kenneth Walker's wife thought Gurdjieff a magician. It also makes it clear that his 'magical' powers were not of the kind that we normally associate with notorious 'occultists' or magicians, like Madame Blavatsky or Aleister Crowley. There are stories of Madame Blavatsky causing raps to resound from all over the room, of Crowley somehow causing men to go on all fours and howl like dogs; but never of their producing this wholly tonic effect on someone. It is not even necessary to assume that Gurdjieff revitalized Peters by some form of telepathic transfer of energy; a psychologist would probably argue that he did it by some form of suggestion.

 As to Gurdjieff's power to renew his own energies, its essence had been understood by psychologists of the nineteenth century, decades before the age of Freud and Jung. William James speaks about it in an important essay called 'The Energies of Man'.

Everyone is familiar with the phenomenon of feeling more or less alive on different days. Everyone knows on any given day that there are energies slumbering in him which the incitements of that day do not call forth, but which he might display if these were greater. Most of us feel as if a sort of cloud weighed upon us, keeping us below our highest notch of clearness in discernment, sureness in reasoning, or firmness in deciding. Compared with what we ought to be, we are only half awake. Our fires are damped, our drafts are checked. We are making use of only a small part of our possible mental and physical resources. In some persons this sense of being cut off from their rightful resources is extreme, and we then get the formidable neurasthenic and psychasthenic conditions, with life grown into one tissue of impossibilities, that so many medical books describe.

Stating the thing broadly, the human individual thus lives far within his limits; he possesses powers of various sorts which he habitually fails to use. He energizes below his *maximum*, and he behaves below his *optimum*. In elementary faculty, in co-ordination, in power of *inhibition* and control, in every conceivable way, his life is contracted like the field of vision of an hysteric subject – but with less excuse, for the poor hysteric is diseased, while in the rest of us, it is only an inveterate *habit* – the habit of inferiority to our full self – that is bad.

James cites the well-known phenomenon of 'second wind' as an example of this power to draw upon vital reserves. When we are completing some task, he says, we make a practice of stopping once we feel tired – once we encounter the first layer of fatigue. If we *force ourselves* to press on, a surprising thing happens. The fatigue gets worse, up to a point, then suddenly vanishes, and we feel better than before. He mentions that one of the standard methods of treating 'neurasthenic' patients in the nineteenth century was to bully patients into making a greater effort than usual. 'First comes the very extremity of distress, then follows unexpected relief.' And he adds: 'We live subject to arrest by degrees of fatigue which we have come only from habit to obey.'

In this sentence, James has defined the essence of Gurdjieff's lifework. It is true that the ideas of Gurdjieff cover an immense range – of psychology, philosophy, cosmology, even alchemy. But at the core of his work lies this notion that we possess greater powers than we realize, and that our apparent limitations are due to a peculiar form of laziness – a laziness that has become so habitual that it has developed into a *mechanism*.

And how can this mechanism be controlled or de-activated?

In his essay on vital reserves, William James points out that we call upon these deeper powers when we are stimulated either by crisis, or by some deep sense of urgency – of purpose. He quotes Colonel Baird-Smith, who was in charge of the defence of Delhi during its six week siege by Indian mutineers in 1857. His mouth was filled with sores and his body covered with them; a wounded ankle was a black, festering mess; diarrhoea had worn him to a shadow. Unable to eat, he lived almost entirely on brandy. Yet it seemed to have no effect on him. The crisis – the need to protect the lives of women and children – kept him in such a state of concentrated determination that he remained alert and energetic during the whole siege. Clearly, *he* did precisely what Gurdjieff did when he left Fritz Peters sitting in the kitchen: reached down inside himself, and summoned vital reserves.

In fact, this method – of deliberately seeking out stimulation, excitement, even crisis – is one of our favourite human devices for escaping that sense of 'a cloud weighing upon us'. A depressed housewife goes and buys herself a new hat. A bored man gets drunk. A discontented teenager steals a car or takes his knuckledusters to a a football match. Generally speaking, the greater a person's potentiality for achievement, the greater his or her objection to that feeling of being 'cut off from one's rightful resources'. Shaw's Captain Shotover tells Ellie Dunne, 'At your age, I looked for hardship, danger, horror and death, that I might feel the life in me more intensely.' And this is clearly the motivation that drove Ernest Hemingway, for example, to spend so much of his time big game hunting, bullfighting, working as a war correspondent.

This desire to break the bonds of their own laziness may even lead men to behave in ways that are obviously contrary to their best interests. Van Gogh threw up a comfortable job as an art dealer to become a lay preacher among the miners in Belgium. Lawrence of Arabia refused comfortable govern-ment appointments to become an ordinary aircraftman in the R.A.F. The philosopher Wittgenstein gave away an inherited fortune to become a badly paid schoolmaster. These 'outsiders' were driven by a need to escape a feeling of enstiflement, of stagnation. The aim was to throw off the 'habit neurosis' – the 'habit of inferiority to one's full self'.

But then, there is obviously an element of absurdity in

deliberately seeking out danger or discomfort, since we otherwise spend so much of our lives trying to avoid them. There *must* be other ways of breaking through to our vital reserves, apart from risking our necks or sleeping on a bed of nails. For example, it is plain that it is not the crisis itself that creates the flow of vital energy; it is our response to it. It is as if some inner-voice gave an *order* that causes something inside us to snap to attention. Colonel Baird-Smith's response to the mutiny was to order himself to keep going, to ignore pain and starvation, until the crisis had been brought under control. The mutiny only instilled him with a sense of the seriousness of the situation, to which his 'vital reserves' responded. And if a man could generate that sense of seriousness, of the need for effort, then he ought to be able to summon the energies without the need for an Indian mutiny.

How is this to be done? According to Gurdjieff, the answer falls into two parts. First of all, a man must commit himself wholly and totally to the task of escaping his normal limitations; it requires the kind of commitment that made saints sit on top of pillars. Secondly, he must understand something of the workings of this complicated computer that houses the human spirit. (Gurdjieff died before the age of computers, so he used the word 'machine'; but he would undoubtedly have found 'computer' more convenient and accurate.) 'Understand the machine.' This body is a computer; so is this brain. Like all computers, they are capable of a far wider range of response than we ever demand of them. But wider responses can only be obtained when they are thoroughly understood.

Gurdjieff's method of securing the first of these two objectives was simply to demand an unusual level of commitment. When the eleven-year-old Fritz Peters told him that he wanted to know 'everything about man', Gurdjieff asked him with great intensity: 'Can you promise to do something for me?' When Peters said yes, Gurdjieff gestured at the vast expanse of lawns of the Chateau du Prieuré, and told him that he must cut them all once a week.

'He struck the table with his fist for a second time. "You must promise on your God." His voice was deadly serious. "You must promise me that you will do this thing no matter what happens . . . Must promise you will do no matter what happens, no matter who try to stop you."' And Peters adds: 'I would have died, if necessary, in the act of mowing the lawns.'

In fact, Gurdjieff then made him work harder and harder, until he was mowing all the lawns in four days.

The principle here is similar to that of commando training: that is, the trainee is made to tackle more and more difficult obstacles, until he can cascade down cliffs on his back and eat barbed wire for breakfast. This was the basis of Gurdjieff's method. But it was not simply a matter of developing strength and alertness. Hard work can become a mere habit, like any other. Gurdjieff's aim was also to persuade his pupils *not* to develop habits. Habit arises from doing something mechanically, with the mind 'elsewhere'. Gurdjieff's pupils were made to work hard; but it was important that they should maintain 'mindfulness', intense awareness.

At some fairly early stage in his career – which we shall consider at greater length in the next chapter – Gurdjieff became acquainted with certain types of eastern dancing that demanded an extraordinary complexity of movements. Anyone who tries patting the head with one hand and rubbing the stomach with the other will know how difficult it is. Gurdjieff devised dances in which the student had to do something not only with both hands, but with both feet and the head as well. Again, these dances became fundamental to training in 'the work'. Their aim was to widen and extend the range of the body's possibilities – what Gurdjieff called 'the moving centre'. It is true that these dances (or 'movements') could, in themselves, become habitual. But, under certain circumstances, they could also be amazingly effective in producing new modes of consciousness. One of the most striking examples is to be found in J. G. Bennett's autobiography *Witness*, describing Bennett's experiences with Gurdjieff at Fontainebleau (the Prieuré) in 1923.

Bennett was suffering from dysentery, contracted in the east.

Each morning, it was harder and harder to get out of bed, and my body shrank from the heavy work in the heat of the sun. The constant diarrhoea made me very weak, but somehow I kept going.

Finally, a day came when I simply could not stand up. I was shaking with fever and very wretched in myself; feeling that I had failed. Just as I was saying to myself: 'I will stay in bed today,' I felt my body rising. I dressed and went to work as usual, but this time with a queer sense of being held together by a superior Will that was not my own.

We worked as usual all the morning. I could not eat lunch that day, but lay on the ground, wondering if I was going to die. Gurdjieff had just introduced afternoon practices of the exercises out-of-doors under the lime grove. When the pupils began to collect under the lime trees, I joined them.

We started by working on a new exercise of incredible complexity that even the most experienced Russian pupils could not master. The structure of the exercises was drawn on the board in symbols, and head, feet, arms and torso had to follow independent sequences. It was a torture for all of us.

Soon I ceased to be aware of anything but the music and my own weakness. I kept saying to myself: 'At the next change I will stop.' . . . One by one, all the English pupils fell out, and most of the Russian women . . .

Gurdjieff stood watching intently. Time lost the quality of before and after. There was no past and no future, only the present agony of making my body move. Gradually I became aware that Gurdjieff was putting all his attention on me. There was an unspoken demand that was at the same time an encouragement and a promise. I must not give up – if it killed me.

Suddenly, I was filled with the influx of an immense power. My body seemed to have turned into light. I could not feel its presence in the usual ways. There was no effort, no pain, no weariness, not even any sense of weight . . . My own state was blissful beyond anything I had ever known. It was quite different from the ecstasy of sexual union, for it was altogether free and detached from the body. It was exultation in the faith that can move mountains.

All had gone into the house for tea, but I went in the opposite direction towards the kitchen garden, where I took a spade and began to dig. Digging in the earth is a searching test of our capacity for physical effort. A strong man can dig fast for a short time or slowly for a long time, but no one can force his body to dig fast for a long time even if he has exceptional training. I felt the need to test the power that had entered me, and I began to dig in the fierce afternoon heat for more than an hour at a rate that I ordinarily could not sustain for two minutes. My weak, rebellious, suffering body had become strong and obedient. The diarrhoea had ceased and I no longer felt the gnawing abdominal pains that had been with me for days. Moreover, I experienced a clarity of thought that I had only known involuntarily and at rare moments . . . The phrase 'in my mind's eye' took on a new meaning as I 'saw' the eternal pattern of each thing I looked at, the trees, the water flowing in the canal and even the spade, and lastly my own body . . . I remember saying aloud: 'Now I see why God hides Himself from us.' But even now I cannot recall the intuition behind this exclamation.

Bennett went for a walk in the forest, and encountered Gurdjieff, who began to speak about man's need for 'higher emotional energy' if he is to transform himself. He went on: 'There are some people in the world, but they are very rare, who are connected to a Great Reservoir or Accumulator of this energy . . . Those who can draw upon it can be a means of helping others.' The implication was clearly that Gurdjieff himself was such a person, and that he had 'supplied' Bennett with the necessary energy for his mystical experience. He added: 'What you have received today is a taste of what is possible for you. Until now you have only known about these things theoretically, but now you have experience.'

Bennett walked on into the forest; the most important part of his experience was still to come.

A lecture of Ouspensky came into my mind. He had spoken about the very narrow limits within which we can control our functions and added: 'It is easy to verify that we have no control over our emotions. Some people imagine that they can be angry or pleased as they will, but anyone can verify that he cannot be astonished at will.' As I recalled these words, I said to myself: 'I will be astonished.' Instantly, I was overwhelmed with amazement, not only at my own state, but at everything that I looked at or thought of. Each tree was so uniquely itself that I felt that I could walk in the forest for ever and never cease from wonderment. Then the thought of 'fear' came to me. At once I was shaking with terror. Unnamed horrors were menacing me on every side. I thought of 'joy', and I felt that my heart would burst from rapture. The word 'love' came to me, and I was pervaded with such fine shades of tenderness and compassion that I saw that I had not the remotest idea of the depth and the range of love. Love was everywhere and in everything. It was infinitely adaptable to every shade of need. After a time, it became too much for me, it seemed that if I plunged any more deeply into the mystery of love, I would cease to exist. I wanted to be free from this power to feel whatever I chose, and at once it left me.

Bennett obviously attached great importance to Gurdjieff's

remarks on 'the Great Reservoir or Accumulator'. But to someone trying to understand the essence of Gurdjieff's ideas, this is less important than the simple fact that Bennett had achieved such total control over his emotions. For *this* is our central human problem: that we are almost constantly the victims of our emotions, always being swept up and down on a kind of inner-switchback. We possess a certain control over them; we *can* 'direct our thoughts' – or feelings – in such a way as to intensify them. This is certainly our most remarkable human characteristic: imagination. Animals require actual physical stimuli to trigger their experience. A man can retreat into a book – or a daydream – and live through certain experiences quite independent of the physical world. He can even, for example, imagine a sexual encounter, and not only experience all the appropriate physical responses, but even the sexual climax. Such a curious ability is far beyond the power of any animal.

Yet our experience of imagination convinces us that it is bound, by its very nature, to be no more than a dim carbon copy of 'real' experience. And the consequences of this unconscious assumption are far greater than we realize. It means that we assume that the world of mind is very much a second best when compared with the world of physical actuality, a kind of sham, a make-believe. So when confronted by some painful emotion, or some physical problem, our natural tendency is to retreat and surrender. We are subject to arrest, not only from degrees of fatigue that we have come to obey by habit, but from degrees of self-pity and boredom. Bennett's experience suggests that, if only we made the effort, we could achieve a degree of control over our feelings that would at present strike us as miraculous. The novelist Proust experienced, for a few seconds, an intense consciousness of the reality of his own past – he describes it in *Swann's Way* – and he spent the remainder of his life trying to rediscover that curious power. Yet such a glimpse would have been a mere by-product of the kind of control that Bennett experienced. To actually *know* this consciously, to realize that we were not intended to reach breaking point so quickly and easily, would obviously alter a man's whole approach to his life and its problems.

To effect such an alteration in human consciousness was Gurdjieff's central aim.

Two

The Early Years

WHO WAS this man whose air of concentrated power impressed so many of his contemporaries?

One of the first published accounts of Gurdjieff is to be found in a book by J. G. Bennett, *What Are We Living For?*, which appeared in 1949, the year of Gurdjieff's death. Bennett says: 'To those who take an interest in such things it has been known for many years that a remarkable teacher had come to the West in the person of a man reputed to have gained access to sources of knowledge denied to any previous western explorer.' He went on:

> Gurdjieff has passed his eighty-third birthday... He was born in the Caucasus, of an old Greek family which migrated more than a hundred years ago from one of the ancient Greek colonies of Asia Minor. From his early childhood he had opportunities of meeting with a series of remarkable men, from contact with whom he acquired the conviction that something of vital importance was missing from the views about man and the world current in the European science and literature he had been set to study.

In fact, Gurdjieff was nowhere near the age of eighty-three when he died. His passport gave the date of his birth as 28 December 1877; if this is accurate, then he died shortly before his seventy-second birthday. In *The Occult*, I have accepted what seems to me the likelier date of 1873. The date makes a slight difference as far as Gurdjieff's nationality is concerned; if he was born in 1873, then he was a Turkish citizen; if in December 1877, then he was a Russian, since his place of birth, Gumru, fell to the Russians during the Russo-Turkish war of 1877; it was renamed Alexandropol, after the Tsar's father.

Gurdjieff's father was Greek; his mother Armenian. Around 1878, the family moved to the nearby town of Kars; this had been taken by the Russians in 1877, and many of the Turkish inhabitants had been massacred. When Kars became part of Russia, thousands of Turks moved out and thousands of Russians moved in. It is important to realize that Gurdjieff was born into an ethnic melting pot; that is, into the reverse of a secure and settled culture. Conditions like these can create a sense of rootlessness and insecurity; they can also stimulate the will to survive. Gurdjieff was a born survivor.

His father was a carpenter by profession, a 'bard' or professional story-teller by choice. From the beginning Gurdjieff had a deep sense of kinship with the past. His father recited parts of the *Epic of Gilgamesh*. One day, Gurdjieff read in a magazine that archaeologists had discovered ancient tablets of the *Epic* in Babylonia, and he speaks of experiencing 'such an inner excitement that it was as if my future destiny depended on all this.' He was impressed that the verses of the epic, as printed in the magazine, were almost identical to those his father had recited; yet they had been passed on by word of mouth for thousands of years. What matters here is the unstated implication: that in that case, other kinds of ancient knowledge may have also survived in the same way.

Like most children, Gurdjieff was fascinated by the world of the 'occult' and paranormal; but, unlike most children, he also had a certain amount of direct experience in this field. At the house of his tutor, Father Bogachevsky, Gurdjieff watched a 'table rapping' session, in which the table tapped out answers to questions with one of its legs. Gurdjieff was still grief-stricken about the death of a favourite sister, and spent the whole of that night awake, puzzling about the problem of life after death. When Gurdjieff asked his first teacher, Father Borsch, about such matters, Borsch asserted that it was all nonsense; as a result, Gurdjieff found himself doubting the word of a man whom he had previously regarded as the incarnation of wisdom. He borrowed books on the subject, but found no satisfactory answer.

He was also intrigued when a half-witted fortune teller told his aunt that he would have a bad sore on his right side, and would have an accident with a firearm. In fact, the sore had been troubling him for some time, but he had told no one about it. A week later, when he was out duck shooting, Gurdjieff was shot in the leg. As a result, Gurdjieff himself consulted the fortune teller, who sat between two lighted candles and stared for a long time at his thumb nail – in which he saw 'pictures'. These prophecies were also fulfilled, although Gurdjieff does not tell us what they were.

In 1888, Gurdjieff heard the sound of a child screaming; he found that a group of children had drawn a circle around a Yezidi boy (the Yezidis were a religious sect, generally regarded as devil worshippers), and the boy was unable to break his way out of it. As soon as Gurdjieff rubbed out a part of the circle, the child was able to escape. Gurdjieff was fascinated; he went from person to person, asking what the phenomenon could mean. One man told him the children had been playing a joke on him, another that it was simply a form of hysteria. In later years, Gurdjieff tried the experiment with a Yezidi woman; when a circle was drawn round her, she could not move outside it, and it took Gurdjieff and another strong man to drag her out. Gurdjieff also confirmed that when a Yezidi is dragged out of a circle, he falls into a state of catalepsy, which disappears if he is placed inside again. Otherwise, says Gurdjieff, it vanishes after thirteen or twenty-one hours.

One morning, Gurdjieff saw a group of women talking excitedly, and learned from them that a young man who had been buried the day before – under a light covering of earth, according to the Tartar custom – had tried to walk home in the night. Someone had seen him and raised the alarm; neighbours had cut the throat of the corpse and carried it back to the cemetery. (Stories of vampires are current in this part of the world.) Again, Gurdjieff questioned everyone he knew about what it could mean.

Accompanying a group of pilgrims from Alexandropol, to the tomb of a saint on Mount Djadjur, Gurdjieff saw a paralytic crawl on to the tomb of the saint, and then walk away cured. He was equally fascinated when, during a long drought, a priest from Antioch brought a miracle-working icon, and prayed for rain. As the procession was marching back to the town, clouds gathered, and the rain poured down.

In the house next to Gurdjieff, a young married woman was dying of 'galloping consumption'. One morning, just after a doctor had been telling Gurdjieff that the woman would soon be dead, her mother-in-law came to ask permission to gather rose hips in the garden. The Virgin had appeared to her in a dream and told her to boil rose hips in milk and give them to the dying woman. The doctor laughed. But the next morning, Gurdjieff met the 'dying' woman coming out of church; a week later, she was completely cured. The doctor explained that all this was purely a matter of chance.

It looks as if, on the whole, Gurdjieff encountered rather more than his fair share of such odd events as a child and teenager – as if fate intended to steer his highly active intelligence in a definite direction. His family wanted him to become a priest. His first 'tutor', Father Borsch, Dean of the Kars Military School (and, in effect, 'bishop' of the whole region), insisted that priests should also have a certain medical knowledge, since they may be wasting their time trying to cure the soul if the illness lies in the body. Gurdjieff himself had a natural inclination for handicrafts – he enjoyed tinkering with things, taking them to pieces and mending them, repairing household articles that had been broken. He used to earn himself pocket money by travelling to Alexandro-pol and undertaking various repairs. (He went there from shame; he wanted no one in Kars to realize how poor they were.) So his time was divided between theology, medicine, and crafts like shoe repairing or clock mending.

Dean Borsch seems to have laid the foundation of Gurdjieff's life-work with remarks about the general 'laws' of human nature. He pointed out, for example, that many adults fail to grow up because they lack the 'corresponding type of the opposite sex' for their completion. If a person fails to find his or her own type, he is likely to end up with a second-best, who prevents his individuality from maturing. As a result, said the Dean, it is absolutely essential for each person to have beside him the person of the corresponding type of the opposite sex if he is to realize his possibilities. The comment sounds as if it might have been derived from Plato or Goethe, but the Dean attributed it to 'our remote ancestors' – so that, again, it sounded like a piece of ancient wisdom that had been transmitted by word of mouth.

In his early teens – Gurdjieff is never specific about dates – he took a job as a stoker in the railway station at Tiflis. He also formed his first important friendship with someone his own age: a theological student named Sarkis Pogossian, son of a Turkish dyer. According to Gurdjieff, he travelled to Echmiadzin, the Armenian equivalent of Mecca, hoping to find an answer to those questions about the supernatural that were tormenting him. He carried with him a parcel for the young novice, who invited him to share his room.

At this time, Gurdjieff's own orientation was basically religious; he describes visiting all the places of pilgrimage and praying at shrines. (It is important to realize that, under different circumstances, Gurdjieff might have ended as an archimandrite of the Greek orthodox church – or as a highly unorthodox religious teacher like Rasputin.) Later, Pogossian – now on the verge of becoming a priest – came to stay with Gurdjieff in Tiflis. The thought of the priesthood depressed Pogossian, and when Gurdjieff suggested that he should take a job at the station, he immediately agreed – becoming a locksmith. At this point, Gurdjieff spent several months helping to survey the route of a proposed railway between Tiflis and Kars. He supplemented his income by approaching the leading men in towns or villages through which the railway was scheduled to pass, and offering to 'fix' a halting place there. Most of them paid the bribes.

Back in Tiflis, he had enough money to give up his job on the railway and spend his days reading. In long discussions, he and Pogossian had reached the conclusion that there was some 'hidden knowledge' that had come down from ancient times. They had bought piles of old Armenian texts from a local bookseller; now they moved to the ruins of the ancient Armenian capital, Ani, built a hut there, and spent their days in study and discussion.

It must be emphasized that Gurdjieff owed his freedom to take such decisions to the unsettled character of life in that region after the Russo-Turkish war. If he and Pogossian had been born in St Petersburg or Constantinople, they would have found it difficult to avoid being ingested by the 'system' and taking up a respectable profession. In the Asiatic equivalent of the American wild west, nobody cared too much if they ignored their families' plans and pursued strange ideas of their own.

So Gurdjieff and Pogossian were able to spend their days talking, and poking around in the ruins of the ancient city. One day, exploring an underground passage, they uncovered a monk's cell, with some decaying parchments written in ancient Armenian. They returned to Alexandropol to decipher these manuscripts. They turned out to be letters to a certain Father Arem. And one of them referred to certain 'mysteries'; the postscript spoke of a 'Sarmoung Brotherhood' which used to exist at the town of Siranoush; they recognized the name as that of an esoteric brotherhood that, according to one of their books, dated back as far as 2500 B.C. They decided that the parchments dated back to the seventh century A.D., that a city called Nivssi referred to in the parchment was present day Mosul, and that the descendants of the Sarmoung Brotherhood were the present day Aisors. The manuscript stated that the secret school had moved to a valley three days journey from Nivssi. This was not too far away – a few hundred miles due south – and Gurdjieff and Pogossian decided it might be worth seeing whether any traces of the ancient school still existed. All they needed was finance for the expedition, and this was provided by a local committee of Armenian patriots, who had decided to send an expedition to a place called Moush. Pogossian persuaded them to appoint himself and Gurdjieff their representatives; and so Gurdjieff set off on his first journey in search of 'secret knowledge'.

Unfortunately, Gurdjieff preferred not to be specific about what he learned. He tells us (in *Meetings With Remarkable Men*) that he and Pogossian went south, disguising themselves for much of the journey as Caucasian Tartars. (They heard rumours that Englishmen had been flayed alive by Aisors for trying to copy inscriptions.) At one point, Pogossian was bitten by a poisonous spider; Gurdjieff cut out the poison with a knife but the wound festered. An Armenian priest, to whom they had to deliver a letter, put them up in his house for a month. He told Gurdjieff a story about an old map he possessed – a Russian prince had offered to buy it for £500, and had finally paid £200 in order to be allowed to copy it. Gurdjieff asked to see the map, and was immensely excited to find that it was an ancient map of Egypt. When the priest was out, he and Pogossian managed to get hold of the map and copied it – Gurdjieff admits that it was immoral, but felt it was necessary. Later, at Smyrna, Gurdjieff and Pogossian got involved in a brawl between two groups of sailors, and both received minor injuries. The next day, at the harbour, they were recognized by the grateful sailors, who proved to be English. When they learned that Gurdjieff and Pogossian wanted to get to Alexandria, two of them went off to try and arrange it. The consequence was that Gurdjieff and Pogossian sailed on an English warship to Egypt, Gurdjieff polishing the brass while Pogossian worked in the engine room. Pogossian decided to go on to Liverpool with the ship, where he became an engineer; Gurdjieff went to Egypt, then on to Jerusalem, where he became a professional guide to Russian tourists. But we are not told whether he and Pogossian found their Sarmoung Brotherhood, or whether Gurdjieff made important discoveries by means of his map of 'pre-sand Egypt'. But he does tell of a curious coincidence. Sitting at the foot of one of the pyramids – this was his second visit to Egypt – looking at his copy of the map, he looked up to observe a grey-haired man standing over him; the man asked, in great excitement, where Gurdjieff had obtained the map. He turned out to be the prince who had paid the Armenian priest £200 to copy it; his name was Prince Yuri Lubovedsky. He and Gurdjieff became close friends.

Bennett believes that Gurdjieff eventually found his Sarmoung Brotherhood – or its modern descendants. Bennett himself tracked down the 'valley three days' ride from Nivssi', and concluded it was a place called Sheik Adi, chief sanctuary of the Yezidis. Gurdjieff also mentions that the Brotherhood had a centre in the 'Olman' monastery in the northern Himalayas, where, he says, he spent three months. And it seems possible that it was there that Gurdjieff eventually discovered the secrets that he would one day pass on to his pupils.

In case the reader is, by this time, beginning to entertain the impression that Gurdjieff may have been a great leg-puller, and that he invented the amazing story of his 'search for truth', let me cite an anecdote that demonstrates his possession of esoteric knowledge. In *Meetings With Remarkable Men*, he tells the story of his acquaintance with a talented Russian girl, Vitvitskaia. She told Gurdjieff how she had always been fascinated by the effect of music, believing that it produces its impressions by means of vibrations, which somehow act upon the biological vibrations of our bodies. In an Afghan monastery she learned how to produce certain effects on an audience by playing definite notes on the piano. Gurdjieff himself was able to confirm some of her theories by telling how he had seen, among the Essenes, a plant made to grow from its seed in half an hour by means of ancient Hebrew music.

In his *Childhood With Gurdjieff*, Fritz Peters tells how a Russian family came to the Prieuré. Gurdjieff told his followers that he could see that their daughter was susceptible to definite musical chords, and that if a certain chord was played, she would fall into a trance. The unsuspecting girl came into the room; Gurdjieff asked his pianist, Hartmann, to play the piano. As he played the stated chord, the girl fainted, and it took a long time to revive her. Gurdjieff persuaded her to repeat the demonstration several times; on each occasion, Peters noticed her bewilderment and hysteria on waking up, and was convinced that there was no possibility of collusion.

This, then, was the kind of knowledge Gurdjieff was seeking – a knowledge that would bring power over people. But he was not interested in the power for its own sake. He wanted to know *why* a Yezidi boy could be confined within a 'magic circle', why a certain chord could send a girl into a trance. Vitvitskaia revealed part of the answer when she told Gurdjieff about the secrets she had learned from the 'Mono-psyche Brethren'. 'It cannot be denied that when the people present corresponded absolutely to the mentioned conditions, I could call forth at will in all of them laughter, tears, malice, kindness, and so on . . .' That is, their emotions could be *triggered*, as if they were machines. This was perhaps the most important single conviction that Gurdjieff gained from his study of esoteric religions: that man is almost entirely mechanical. He believes that he 'lives' because he laughs, cries, gets angry, feels sorrow. In fact, says Gurdjieff, such reactions are little more than computerized responses to certain definite stimuli, mere reflexes. This is the meaning of the title of one of Bennett's books about Gurdjieff: *Is There Life on Earth?* The answer is: very little. Most of what we call life is mechanical response.

But can we achieve a degree of freedom from our mechanisms? When people asked Gurdjieff that question, he told them that they had just taken the most important step towards developing free will.

Vitvitskaia's discovery about music clearly reveals that the 'machine' is controlled by vibrations – in this case, musical vibrations. And this insight was confirmed when Gurdjieff spent some time in a 'Sarmoung' monastery in Turkestan. He and his friend Soloviev were taken there blindfold, and had to swear that they would never reveal its whereabouts, even if they could guess it. There Gurdjieff again saw Prince Lubovedsky – for the last time. Lubovedsky took him to the Women's Court in the monastery, to witness the sacred dances. There he saw a number of peculiar 'apparatuses', whose purpose was to teach the priestesses the basic postures of the sacred dances. Each apparatus, says Gurdjieff, consisted of a column standing on a tripod. From this column, in different places, there projected seven 'branches' or arms. Each arm, in turn, was divided in seven parts, the individual parts connected together by ball-and-socket joints, like a man's shoulder joint. There was also a cupboard full of plates, each one containing a mysterious inscription. These inscriptions were instructions for altering the position of the 'arms'. The positions were the basic alphabet of various postures and movements of the sacred dances. Gurdjieff says that when he saw these dances, 'I was astounded, not by the sense and meaning contained in their dances, which I did not as yet understand, but by the external precision and exactitude with which they performed them.' These dances were obviously the basis of the movements he taught his pupils. (Having seen them performed by Bennett's pupils at Sherborne House in Gloucestershire, I can confirm that their precision and exactitude rivet the attention, producing a strange aesthetic effect.)

But the point to note here is the *number* of the arms and their segments – seven times seven. As we shall see, the technical aspect of Gurdjieff's teaching depends on the notion of 'octaves' (i.e. the seven notes of the scale, completed by a return to the first note.) He asserts that the universe consists of seven levels of creation, which are also seven levels of vibration. (This notion of vibrations is central to Gurdjieff's thinking.) Man is subject to the 'law of seven'. Man also has seven 'minds', or centres, of which the intellectual mind is the lowest – or at least, the clumsiest. (There is also a moving centre – governing the body – an emotional centre, a sex centre, an instinctive centre, and also a higher emotional and higher thinking centre.) He is also subject to another law, the law of three, which asserts that all action is the result of three forces (and not, as science declares, of two.) The first two forces, positive and negative, merely counterbalance one another; they require a kind of kick from a third force. It seems plain that the tripod at the base of the column was intended to symbolize this law of three.

In short, it looks as if Gurdjieff derived most of his important basic principles from the Sarmoung monasteries in which he was accepted as a pupil. We may say that his quest began in the underground monk's cell in the ruined city of Ani, and ended in the Sarmoung monastery in the Himalayas. Gurdjieff's account of his search is fragmentary, and sometimes confused. He states that he was one of a group who called themselves 'Seekers After Truth', headed by Prince Lubovedsky; but the part played by these other 'seekers' in *Meetings With Remarkable Men* seems to be minimal. But perhaps his most important pronouncement is one that occurs in his first book *Herald of Coming Good*, where he states that after spending some time in a Sufi monastery in central Asia, he came to the conclusion that the answers to his questions 'can be found . . . in the sphere of man's unconscious mentation' – meaning his unconscious mind. That is to say, the real answers are already there, inside us, and can only be discovered by minute self-observation, and by reasoning about and analysing what we observe.

So for practical purposes, we may ignore the remainder of Gurdjieff's 'search', which took him to various places in Asia. *Meetings With Remarkable Men* gives us a clear picture of these early days, but it should be read with caution. One whole section, describing how the 'Seekers of Truth' went in search of a lost city in the Gobi desert (taking twenty-foot stilts with them so they could walk above the sand storms) seems to be pure fiction – Bennett thinks it is probably an allegory of people who search for truth 'out there' instead of 'in here'. There is no knowing how much of the book is invention. Its chief value lies in the fact that it is the most accessible and readable of Gurdjieff's four books, and that it gives us an excellent picture of Gurdjieff as a real human being. He is never averse to describing the various dubious ways in which he made money – like catching sparrows, dyeing them different colours, and selling them as 'American canaries'.

And his stories of his various companions – even of his dog –
show him to have been a generous and warm-hearted man, a
view confirmed by all who knew him well. But it seems
unlikely that we shall ever know precisely what Gurdjieff did
between 1891, when he set out on his adventures (either at
the age of fourteen or nineteen, depending which date of
birth we accept) until about 1910, when he first appears in
Moscow and St Petersburg as a teacher of self-knowledge. It
seems fairly certain there was an intervening period when
Gurdjieff became a professional hypnotist and wonder-
worker – what his critics would doubtless describe as a
charlatan. In the Ekim Bey chapter of *Meetings With Remarkable
Men*, he describes how he and Ekim Bey (the man who taught
him about hypnotism) earned some badly-needed money in
Tashkent by hiring a hall and putting on a 'magical' show of
hypnotism and other phenomena. An extraordinary photograph in Bennett's *Gurdjieff: Making a New World* shows a
young Gurdjieff (with hair) 'as Professional Hypnotist',
standing against some kind of a stage backdrop and looking
like the villain in a Victorian pantomime. Bennett surmises
that Gurdjieff's 'professional' period lasted from about 1907
until 1910.

But the most important event of these early years occurred
around 1904, near a town on the edge of the Gobi desert; it is
described in his last book *Life is Real Only Then, When 'I Am'*.
Gurdjieff's health had been breaking down for some time – in
fact, since the year 1896, when he had been hit by a stray
bullet on the island of Crete, then decided to walk back to
Russia. In 1902, a second 'stray bullet' brought him close to
death; he was unconscious for three months at a place on the
edge of the Gobi desert, near Yangihissar. Two years later, he
made the mistake of getting between the Tsar's soldiers and a
group of revolutionaries; a third stray bullet again came close
to ending his life. By an odd coincidence, he again found
himself convalescing in the same place on the edge of the
Gobi desert.

One evening, when he was physically recovered, Gurdjieff
lay in the moonlight, thinking over the past few years. His
reflections plunged him into gloom; in fact, his own short-
comings struck him as so appalling that he experienced a
sense of total worthlessness. The negative current of his
thought was so powerful that he was unable to shake himself

free; he felt he was about to lose consciousness when the movement of the camels distracted him and enabled him to throw off this 'dark night of the soul'. Lying next to a spring, he began a process of self-examination. It seemed that the various 'powers' he had acquired in the past few years had been used for the gratification of his worst impulses, self-love, vanity, pride, sexual lust. According to Gurdjieff, his powers 'had been brought to such a level that by only a few hours of self-preparation I could from a distance of ten miles kill a yak; or, in twenty-four hours, could accumulate life forces of such compactness that I could in five minutes put to sleep an elephant.' Yet in spite of these semi-magical powers, he still felt himself to be little better than a machine. He was still unable to maintain a state of self-remembering (intense self-awareness) for more than a few seconds.

What could he do to increase his self-awareness, to galvanize his inner being with a sense of urgency? The saints of old tried sleeping on beds of nails and wearing hair shirts; Gurdjieff had also tried such 'mechanical' disciplines, and found them insufficient. The only way, he decided, was to make some enormous sacrifice. (An inveterate smoker might, for example, give up tobacco, so that the misery of his deprivation would continually serve as a kind of 'alarm clock'.) What could he sacrifice? 'Thinking and thinking, I came to the conclusion that if I should intentionally stop utilizing the exceptional power in my possession . . . then there must be forced out of me such a reminding source.' In short, he would sacrifice his powers of hypnotism and telepathy.

'As soon as I realized the sense of this idea, I was as if reincarnated; I got up and began to run around the spring . . . like a young calf.'

Gurdjieff thereupon took an oath never again to use his powers merely for self-gratification – only for 'scientific' purposes.

It was at this point that he ceased to be a mere 'magician' – like his contemporary Aleister Crowley – and became primarily a teacher. It was the beginning of a new era in his life.

Three

Moscow and St Petersburg

IN THE year 1909, Gurdjieff decided that it was time to embark on his new career as a teacher. The reason, he explains in his first book, *Herald of Coming Good*, was that 'there was, among men, a widely prevalent ... psychosis', known as occultism or spiritualism. He was, at this period, in Tashkent (now in Soviet Central Asia). There, as in Moscow and St Petersburg, there was a feverish interest in all forms of occultism and mysticism, in the doctrines of Madame Blavatsky and Rudolf Steiner, in seances and table-rapping and spirit-healing. And no doubt Gurdjieff reflected that he knew more about 'hidden knowledge' than all the fashionable occultists and mystics put together.

At all events, he began to frequent spiritualist and theo-sophical circles. He says:

> The ensuing circumstances of my life were so favourable to me that, within six months, I succeeded not only in coming into contact with a great number of these people, but even in being accepted as a well-known 'expert' and guide in evoking so-called 'phenomena of the beyond' in a very large circle.

In a short time, he says, he was regarded as a great maestro of all supernatural knowledge. He speaks frankly of his 'skill in producing tricks', so it seems likely that not all the 'psychic manifestations' he obtained were genuine. His aim, at this point, was to form a circle of disciples who were genuinely in search of power over themselves – not the kind of hysterical enthusiasts who were at that time following Rasputin in St Petersburg. His aim, he explains, was to be able to 'put into the lives of people what I had already learned.' That is to say, he wanted to put his ideas to the test. He regarded his students as 'guinea pigs'.

His success was apparently very considerable – so much so that he ended by organizing no less than three groups in three different cities – he does not specify which these were. We know nothing of Gurdjieff at this period – none of the written accounts by disciples date back this far. Gurdjieff himself says that he decided to wind up his Tashkent venture because the people all tended to belong to only three or four different types, and that he felt that genuine success could only be obtained if his groups contained representatives of *all* human types. (He says there are twenty-eight.) So in the year 1912, he decided to move to Russia.

The move may have been decided as a result of a decision he took on 13 September – he gives the exact date in *Herald of Coming Good*. On this date, he says, he took an oath to spend the next twenty-one years leading 'in some ways an artificial life, modelled upon a programme which had previously been planned in accordance with certain definite principles.'

What exactly did he mean by 'an artificial life'? Bennett rightly says that most of the people who met Gurdjieff felt that he was in some way 'hiding himself'. People who came to know him well – insofar as anyone ever did – had the feeling that he was *acting a part*, never responding to people in a direct and spontaneous manner. Yet disciples like Ouspensky had no doubt that this was not because he had anything to hide. It was because he felt that he could only achieve certain results by approaching his pupils in an objective manner, as a doctor approaches the patient, and aiming to produce certain effects on them. (Modern psychologists do this a great deal – perhaps telling their subjects that they will experience a certain response, to see whether they will convince themselves that they have received a non-existent stimulus. Lying to the subject is an essential part of such an experiment.) After two years of 'teaching' in Tashkent, Gurdjieff may have felt that a new relationship to his pupils was necessary: not that of Master and disciples, but something closer to a scientist and his assistants.

In addition to organizing his groups, Gurdjieff was also engaged in many business enterprises: he lists government contracts for supplying and constructing railways and roads, dealing in cattle (as his father had before he became a carpenter), and running stores, restaurants and cinemas. He also carried on a trade in carpets and antiques. In 1912, he sold his various businesses, realizing more than a million roubles, and moved to Moscow. There he purchased an estate, and prepared to set up his Institute for the Harmonious Development of Man.

Historically speaking, he was unlucky. He had spent fifteen years seeking 'hidden knowledge', and another three years making a fortune; now he was ready to launch his institute – to consolidate his life's work – just at the time when Europe was about to plunge into the most disastrous and widespread war of all time. Gurdjieff was apparently unaware of the international situation; he later said that he chose Russia because it was 'peaceful, rich and quiet'. His years in Asia and Africa had given him no inkling of what was to come.

Bennett is convinced that Gurdjieff moved in court circles in these years and that he met the Tsar. Certainly, he was the kind of person who might have exerted a wholly beneficial influence on Russian politics in this period. Bennett suggests that he was associated with a moderate party surrounding the Tsar and that he was 'canvassed as a counter to the hated Rasputin'. The remark shows a lack of knowledge of Russian politics during this epoch. Rasputin himself had little or no influence over the Tsar at this period, although the Tsarina continued to believe in him – his drunkenness and indiscretions had led to his fall from favour. Insofar as Rasputin *was* an influence, it was for liberalism and reasonableness. (He made enormous exertions to dissuade the Tsar from going to war in 1914.) So there could be no question of Gurdjieff being a 'counter influence'. At all events, Gurdjieff was sufficiently close to the court to become acquainted with one of the Tsarina's ladies in waiting, Countess Ostrowska, whom he married.

And now, at last, it becomes possible to draw upon first hand accounts of meetings with Gurdjieff. The earliest of these seems to be a 'story' or essay called 'Glimpses of Truth',* written by one of Gurdjieff's Moscow disciples in 1914 (with

*Included in *Views from the Real World*, London 1973.

Gurdjieff's encouragement), and referring to the period when Gurdjieff first came to Moscow. The anonymous author tells how, at a certain period of his life, he became interested in occultism, no doubt reading books on the Qabalah, the Tarot, and so on. He pursued his search with an enthusiasm which seems peculiarly Russian. (Berdyaev tells a story of how, at five o'clock in the morning, one member of a discussion group remarked: 'We can't go to bed yet – we haven't decided whether God exists.') A friend, whom he calls A., was equally absorbed in the quest for esoteric knowledge. Then the friend seemed to lose interest; he had, unknown to the author, met Gurdjieff.

One day, the writer noticed an advertisement in a Moscow newspaper for a ballet called 'The Struggle of the Magicians'. The author was named as G. I. Gurdjieff. When he mentioned this to A., his friend revealed – with some reluctance – that he knew Gurdjieff, and agreed to try and arrange a meeting.

On a Sunday afternoon, A. rang up. 'Be at the railroad at seven o'clock. We are going to see Mr Gurdjieff.' The writer felt that this was inconvenient – he had important business. But he decided to put it off, and arrived on time. His acquaintance was waiting, and they took a train to a 'country resort near Moscow'. On the way there, A. told him something about Gurdjieff – how he had spent years wandering in the East, and had now decided to set up an Institute near Moscow. This account also contains the inaccurate statement that Gurdjieff had come to Russia two or three years earlier and lived in St Petersburg. Typically, Gurdjieff never corrected this, although he allowed 'Glimpses of Truth' to circulate among his pupils.

From the station, a sleigh drove them to the gates of a country house. They went in the front door, passed through a completely dark antechamber, hung with heavy curtains, and came into a room where a middle-aged man was sitting on a low ottoman, smoking a water pipe.

It is worth recounting these preliminaries, for they are, as we shall see, typical of Gurdjieff's way of meeting prospective pupils – the abrupt telephone call 'Be at so and so'. It was designed not so much to intrigue as to filter out those who lacked enthusiasm and determination.

Gurdjieff, says the writer, had an oriental complexion. 'His eyes particularly attracted my attention, not so much in themselves as by the way he looked at me, not as if he saw me for the first time, but as though had known me long and well.' The walls and floor were covered with rare oriental carpets, and the ceiling with beautiful silk shawls; the light came from a huge glass globe resembling a lotus flower. It sounds as if Gurdjieff was out to create the correct 'mystical' atmosphere. But his conversation turned out to be oddly concrete and down to earth – a fact that impressed most 'seekers' who met him. He spoke Russian badly and hesitantly (his native languages being Greek and Armenian).

Gurdjieff began with a discourse on the Hermetic formula 'As above, so below', illustrating it with the life of man, then with the life of the earth itself, then moving to the solar system. He spoke of the Law of Three – the three forces, action, resistance and equipoise. All this, understandably, left the occultist slightly breathless.

Gurdjieff continued with an outline of his basic 'cosmological' (as opposed to psychological) system. Since, in this book, I shall be more concerned with Gurdjieff's psychological ideas, it will be convenient to offer a brief outline of his cosmology at this point.

According to Gurdjieff, the universe is a living organism, which consists of seven levels, the highest of which is the supreme intelligence. These levels can be thought of as a ladder down which energy is transmitted, changing its nature as it moves from level to level. In this sense, Gurdjieff's scheme resembles that of the Qabalah, whose Tree of Life could also be thought of as a kind of ladder which winds and twists as it ascends from man (at the bottom) to God (at the top). The 'levels', of course, are realms of spiritual reality, not physical worlds. But because of the law 'As above, so below', they can be regarded as physical worlds. For this reason, Gurdjieff identifies his seven levels with bodies in the universe: the moon, the earth, the planets, the sun, the galaxy, the totality of worlds, and the absolute. The moon is at the lowest level, and anyone who lives on that level is subject to no less than ninety-six laws. Men on earth are subject only to forty-eight laws. The planets are subject to twenty-four. The absolute is subject to only one law – its own. Gurdjieff calls this scheme 'the ray of creation'. Those who find it incomprehensible are advised not to worry; the essence of Gurdjieff's ideas can be grasped without it.

Equally important in Gurdjieff's cosmology is the notion of the notes of the octave. This is, basically, the major law governing our human activity. Everyone must have noticed that we seldom reach the long-term objectives we have set for ourselves. We make some important resolution and decide to carry it out with determination, step by step. And for a short time, we carry on in an undeviating straight line towards our goal. And then, without noticing it, we lose that original drive, and change our direction slightly. Then later we again change our direction. Sometimes we do this so often that we end up doing the exact reverse of what we set out to do. (This explains, for example, why so many fighters for political freedom end up as bullies and tyrants.)

The reason, says Gurdjieff, lies in the law of the octave. In terms of vibrations, there are two places in the octave which are 'weaker' than elsewhere – the space between *Mi* and *Fa*, and between *Ti* and *Do*; there are semitones between these notes, instead of full tones. And where our energies are concerned, these are the points where, unless we are deliberately *reinforced*, we change direction.

Creative processes depend on descending octaves. For example, in writing this book, I began by contemplating the whole of Gurdjieff's thought, and planning it into seven chapters. If I had possessed some computer that could instantly translate my vision into words, this book could have been written in ten minutes. But after it had been subdivided into seven sections, I then had to decide what to put into each section and what to leave out. If the final version of this book is anything at all like my original conception, it will only be because I have applied the law of octaves, and deliberately *reinforced* that original stimulus at certain definite points. That is, I have broken off, and carefully re-thought what I was doing. Every writer – or artist or musician – is thoroughly familiar with the process I am describing. This is why a painter keeps standing back to look at his canvas, then goes away to sleep on it and comes back to it afresh the next day. A work of art cannot be created in one long, continuous burst of application; if the artist ignores this rule, his work becomes, quite literally, broken-backed. (This is why so many of Balzac's novels start off so magnificently and end so badly.)

All these laws are outlined to the author of 'Glimpses of Truth'. After this, Gurdjieff explains that the body can be compared to a factory with three storeys, the head, the chest and the abdomen. These function on different kinds of 'food'. The stomach needs meat and drink; the chest needs air, while the brain needs impressions. This was an important part of Gurdjieff's doctrine – that impressions and experiences are just as much 'food' as bread is, and that we would starve without them. Experiments in sensory deprivation, using a black room, have shown the literal truth of his observation; but in 1912, such experiments were unknown, and his assertion sounded bizarre and unfounded. It is one of many such examples of the startling accuracy of his insights. The three kinds of 'food', says Gurdjieff, belong to different octaves.

He ended by telling the new disciple something about his ballet 'The Struggle of the Magicians', explaining that it was intended primarily to entertain, but that it also contained certain sacred dances whose meanings related to the Law of Three and the Law of Seven. (We have already seen how Gurdjieff learned about these dances – and laws – in the Sarmoung monastery.) Gurdjieff was scathing about most contemporary art, explaining that it is purely subjective, a mere reflection of the neuroses of the individual artist. *Objective* art is a different matter, since it attempts to convey the same universal meaning to all.

The 'story' ends with A. drawing the blinds, and revealing that it is daylight – in fact, nine o'clock in the morning. Gurdjieff orders a carriage to take them both back to the station. And so the fragment breaks off.

It was through 'The Struggle of the Magicians' that P. D. Ouspensky, Gurdjieff's most influential exponent, became acquainted with the man to whose ideas he was to devote the remainder of his life.

Ouspensky, like Gurdjieff, was a seeker after 'hidden knowledge', and in 1914 he had travelled to India in search of it. He met various teachers who offered to accept him into their schools; but Ouspensky had no desire to settle in India. He returned to Moscow, where he saw a notice about 'The Struggle of the Magicians', and wrote an unfavourable comment on it for his newspaper. In the spring of 1915 Ouspensky gave several lectures about his search for 'hidden knowledge' to St Petersburg audiences, and two acquaintances he made there told him about the Caucasian Greek who was responsible for 'The Struggle of the Magicians'. Ouspensky was not impressed; Gurdjieff sounded like another mystical charlatan. His first meeting with him changed that impression, but still left him badly puzzled. He was introduced to Gurdjieff in a small café in a back street, 'a man of an oriental type, no longer young [Gurdjieff was about 40] with a black moustache and piercing eyes, who astonished me because he seemed to be disguised and completely out of keeping with the place and its atmosphere.' Gurdjieff spoke with a Caucasian accent – which, to a Russian, would sound rather as a broad Lancashire accent to an Englishman – i.e. hardly associated with profound or subtle ideas.

They spoke of eastern philosophy and the 'search for truth', and Ouspensky quickly realized that Gurdjieff was a man who had experienced most of the things he talked about. At this point, he invited Ouspensky to a meeting of some of his pupils. On the way there, he told Ouspensky of the immense expense he had incurred in hiring the flat where the meeting took place. He also told Ouspensky that many professors and artists in Moscow were interested in his ideas, but when Ouspensky pressed for names, was silent. They arrived at the flat and Ouspensky was embarrassed to find that it was the kind of plain flat that was given to schoolteachers – rent free. Why had Gurdjieff told him the story about his enormous expenses? It was as if Gurdjieff was deliberately trying to confirm Ouspensky's original impression that he was some kind of a confidence trickster.

The 'disciples' seemed to be schoolteachers. One of them read aloud the 'Glimpses of Truth' manuscript, which Ouspensky found confusing and badly written. He asked what system Gurdjieff's pupils were studying, and was told that it was 'work on oneself'. But there was no further elucidation. Moreover, Gurdjieff asked whether the story could be printed in a newspaper, and Ouspensky had to say no – it was too long and had no beginning and end. It sounded as if Gurdjieff was trying to use Ouspensky to get personal publicity.

But later meetings in the same back street café left Ouspensky in no doubt that Gurdjieff possessed real knowledge. He told Ouspensky two things that instantly impressed him: that man is basically a machine, who merely responds to his environment, and that we are mistaken to think that we possess an ego, an individual 'I'. We possess dozens of 'I's', probably thousands. This is why it is so hard to work or behave consistently. One 'I' makes a new year's resolution, but another 'I' takes over a few hours later and decides to break it. This was the kind of down-to-earth psychology that appealed to Ouspensky's basically scientific outlook.

When Gurdjieff told Ouspensky that his Moscow pupils paid a thousand roubles a year, Ouspensky said it sounded a lot. At this, Gurdjieff explained that it was important for his pupils to pay for what they received. First of all, people do not value what they receive too easily; second, people who could not find that much money per year would probably be bad at 'the work'; Gurdjieff emphasized that it is the competent, efficient people, not the neurotic dreamers, who can generate the power to change themselves.

The turning point in their relationship occurred when Ouspensky asked: 'Is it possible to stop being a machine?' Gurdjieff replied: 'If you had asked such questions more often, we might, perhaps, have got somewhere in our talks. It *is* possible to stop being a machine, but for that it is necessary first of all to *know the machine.*'

It might be said that Ouspensky had at last asked the right question. And Gurdjieff had given the right answer. From now on, Ouspensky was wholly committed to learning what Gurdjieff had to teach.

Man is in prison, said Gurdjieff. If he is to have a chance to escape, then he must begin by realizing that he is in prison. Until he has reached this point, he cannot even begin. Then arises the question: how to escape? Here, Gurdjieff made a statement that is also central to his work. A group of people stands a better chance of escape than a single person, for they can collaborate on a tunnel. A man on his own stands little chance. For man is basically *asleep*. He thinks that his everyday consciousness is 'waking consciousness', as opposed to the unconscious state he plunges into every night. This is perhaps his greatest mistake. In fact, when we wake up in the morning, we simply enter another form of sleeping consciousness. We merely react to circumstances, doing today what we did yesterday and the day before. Various things can give us flashes of 'awakening' – a sudden crisis, the prospect of a need to change one's whole mode of existence, even setting out on a journey or a holiday. A mother holding her new baby for the first time may 'wake up' for a moment, and realize, in a flash, that the consciousness she accepts every day of her life is not *necessary*, that life could be completely different, far more fascinating and complex. In short, that she is *free*. But if, ten minutes later, she asks herself: 'What is this freedom?', she has already forgotten.

It may make Gurdjieff's approach easier to understand if instead of speaking about the 'machine', we use the term 'robot'. I have a robot in my unconscious mind who does things for me. When I learn to type, or drive a car, or learn a foreign language, I have to do it painfully and consciously, step by step. Soon, my robot-valet takes over from me, and types or drives much faster and more efficiently than 'I' can. This robot is of incalculable importance. When I was a child, he was far less efficient, and as a result, I was clumsy, and everything cost me far more effort. Now my robot takes most of the work of living off my shoulders.

There is one problem. He not only does the things I want him to do – like typing and talking French. He also does things I *don't* want him to do. I like music and poetry; but when I hear a symphony or read a poem a dozen times or so, it loses half its impact because *the robot is listening* instead of me. If I am preoccupied, he eats my dinner for me. He may even make love to my wife. I miss a great deal of interesting and fresh experience because I have become too dependent on the robot.

Plainly, Gurdjieff is talking about the robot, and our slavery to him. I *can* put the robot out of action, so as to experience the 'newness' of things. A couple of glasses of wine makes the robot relax. Psychedelic drugs like mescalin or LSD completely paralyse the robot, and the result is that the drug-taker is confronted by a blaze of reality that dazzles him; a flower or a tree may seem so real that they arrest the attention, bursting with meaning.

The trouble is that such drugs put the robot completely out of action. And this is not what is required. For we developed the robot in the first place because we wanted *more freedom*. It is not good sense to paralyse him. In fact, in moods of real freedom, the 'real me' and the robot seem to arrive at a perfect accord. William James remarks that a footballer may play the game superbly for years, yet one day, he breaks through some inner barrier, and suddenly he can't put a foot wrong; *the game seems to play him.* Or a musician may suddenly find that he is playing his instrument with a curious perfection, with a degree of control such as he has never achieved before. This, in fact, is what happened to John Bennett in the woods at Fontainebleau – except that his 'instrument' was his own body, his own mind, which could suddenly conjure up any mood he wanted. And *this* kind of freedom could not be achieved through a psychedelic drug. It requires active co-operation between 'the real me' and 'the robot'. Every writer, for example, knows that a glass of alcohol may remove his inhibitions and make him write more freely. Three or four glasses may produce a warm glow in which he feels he can pour a masterpiece on to the typewriter. But when he reads what he has written the next morning, it is nonsense. The wine had removed the inhibitions, but it had also removed the *critical checks* that select the right word, the right expression. Alcohol is no substitute for the kind of hard work that produces the sudden 'break-through', the perfect collaboration of criticism and inspiration, of robot and 'real me'.

Expressed in this way, we can begin to see what Gurdjieff was aiming at. We are talking about William James's 'second wind', about those curious influxes of power in which you feel more alive. How can we hope to produce these at will? By *not* doing things 'automatically', by not drifting through life with our eyes fixed on the outside world. The first step is to LOOK INSIDE, to observe the complex relationship between 'real me' and robot. This is not a way of meditation, or of mysticism, or of physical self-discipline. This is primarily a way of knowledge, a way that depends on knowing *certain definite things.*

Gurdjieff in later life

The Prieuré from the Lime Avenue

Gurdjieff's 'Kosshah' in the Study House at the Prieuré

J. G. Bennett

P. D. Ouspensky

Four

Ouspensky in Search of Miracles

IN THE last years of his life – he died in 1947 – Ouspensky wrote an account of these early days with Gurdjieff under the title *Fragments of an Unknown Teaching*; it was published after his death as *In Search of the Miraculous*. But in 1914, Gurdjieff would have forbidden any such attempt to write about his ideas. New members of the group were sworn to secrecy; they were not even to discuss the ideas among themselves. This was not due to some passion for playing at cloak and dagger. At one of their earliest meetings, Gurdjieff explained to Ouspensky: 'Can a man who does not know himself keep a secret? Of course, he can promise to do so, but can he keep his promise? For he is not one – there are many different people in him. *One in him* promises, and believes that he wants to keep the secret. But tomorrow *another in him* will tell it to his wife, or to a friend over a bottle of wine . . . .' So the demand for secrecy, the curious mystifications, the demand for high fees, were all part of an attempt to force everyone to try to assert a 'controlling ego'.

Gradually, Ouspensky began to understand the motives for at least some of the 'mystifications'. For example, Gurdjieff would come to Petersburg from Moscow about once every two weeks. But he would not allow Ouspensky to fix a meeting in advance. When a meeting *was* held, Gurdjieff would announce that he had to return to Moscow the next morning. But the next day he would say that he had decided to stay until evening. The day would be spent in cafés, where various people would come to see Gurdjieff. Then, not long before the time at which meetings were usually held, Gurdjieff would tell Ouspensky to ring up members of the group and invite them to a meeting that evening. Naturally, most people would already have other engagements, so only a few would turn up. Gurdjieff was quite deliberately creating obstacles. Eventually, there was a small group of people who could all be reckoned on to drop whatever they were doing to attend a meeting, no matter how inconvenient. These were the ones Gurdjieff was interested in. 'People do not value what is easily come by', said the wily old sage.

Ouspensky was also puzzled by Gurdjieff's curious habit of arranging lavish dinners, with huge quantities of food and wine – of which Gurdjieff himself consumed very little. He seemed to want to create the impression of being a gourmand. But those who knew him well could see that this was 'acting'. 'Our feeling of this "acting" in Gurdjieff was exceptionally strong. Among ourselves we often said we never saw him and never would. In any other man so much "acting" would have produced an impression of falsity. In him, "acting" produced an impression of strength . . . .' But Ouspensky adds the heartfelt comment: 'although . . . not always; sometimes there was too much of it'. Even at this early stage, Ouspensky was beginning to feel that Gurdjieff was overdoing it. Eventually, the feeling would cause the break between them.

Ouspensky also noted with mixed feelings Gurdjieff's impish sense of humour. He tells how Gurdjieff would arrive in St Petersburg with a bale of oriental carpets and place an advertisment in a newspaper, which would bring crowds of potential buyers. Ouspensky used to sit and watch the haggling, and noticed how much Gurdjieff enjoyed playing on the weak side of his customers. One rich but tight-fisted lady had selected a dozen expensive carpets, but was haggling over them at some length. Gurdjieff had apparently grown tired of 'acting', for he suddenly offered her every carpet in the room for a quarter of the price of the ones she had selected. She was startled, but immediately began to haggle again. Gurdjieff told her good-humouredly that he would think over her offer overnight – but by the next morning he had returned to Moscow. He obviously wanted to show Ouspensky that people are so mechanical that they often act against their own best interests.

On another occasion, a well-known 'occultist' came to see Gurdjieff and tried to establish a friendship. Gurdjieff looked at him with astonishment and insisted that he was not a guru – merely a carpet seller. He unrolled his carpets and tried to sell him some; the occultist went away convinced that his friends had been pulling his leg. This was not simply self-defence on Gurdjieff's part (the occultist would probably have been a waste of time); it was a delight in manipulating people, playing the puppet-master.

But Ouspensky was impressed by his self-sufficiency. A Persian came to mend carpets, and Ouspensky noticed how intently Gurdjieff was studying the complicated operation, which involved a metal hook. Gurdjieff tried to buy it from him but the Persian declined to sell. The next day, Ouspensky found Gurdjieff sitting cross-legged mending carpets as if he had been doing it all his life; he was using a hook which he had filed from an old penknife.

When Ouspensky asked Gurdjieff whether 'occult' literature might make a good preparation for Gurdjieff's own teaching – Ouspensky was thinking of the Tarot – Gurdjieff made the interesting reply: 'Yes . . . For instance, take yourself: you might already know a great deal if you knew *how to read*. I mean that if you *understood* everything you have read in your life . . . if you understood everything you have written in your own book [*Tertium Organum*] I should come and bow to you and beg you to teach me.' He was making the point that we can know something superficially without grasping its implications – without seeing how it *relates* to other things. And he went on to say: 'What a man knows *well*, that is his preparation [for understanding]. If a man knows how to make coffee well or how to make boots well, then it is already possible to talk to him. The trouble is that nobody knows anything well.' This could be compared with a comment by Hermann Hesse in *Journey to the East*: 'I then discovered how a long time devoted to small details exalts us and increases our strength.' It causes us to *slow down* the mind and allow thought to become permeated with feeling.

At another of these early talks, someone asked Gurdjieff about personal immortality. Gurdjieff's reply was that immortality, like individuality, is a quality that is not naturally possessed by human beings; most people consist of such a crowd of 'I's' that there is little to prevent their total disintegration. Immortality, like individuality, can only be achieved by immense effort.

He went on to say that man consists of four bodies, each one of which is 'finer' than the one before. They are four independent organisms, mutually interpenetrating one another.

The first body is our ordinary physical body. The second is the emotional or astral body (Gurdjieff also called it the natural body). The third is the spiritual body. The fourth is the 'Master', the 'I', the presiding ego. But in most people this fourth body does not exist, or is so undeveloped as to be useless. He compared these four bodies to a horse and carriage. The physical body is the carriage. The emotional body is the horse. The spiritual or mental body is the driver who sits on the box. The 'divine body' or 'I' is the *owner* of the horse and carriage.

The trouble with most human beings is that they are entirely dominated by their bodies. The body is a machine, an automaton driven by external influences which produce physical appetites. These appetites in turn influence our emotions. Our emotions cause certain thoughts to arise in us. And these changing thoughts and desires cause a whole series of conflicting 'I's' to come into existence.

It should be the other way round. A man who has created a real 'I' exercises his will-power, which influences his thoughts, which influence his emotions, which influence his body . . . That is how it *should* be.

At the next talk, Gurdjieff explained that traditional religious disciplines attempt to alter the carriage, horse, and driver. A man who directs all his energy to disciplining his physical body is called a fakir. He might endure incredible sufferings for months or years at a time to subdue the body. The monk prefers to work on his emotions. He fasts and prays and meditates and attempts to subdue his emotions and to fix his mind on God. The man who sets out to discipline the mind itself, and to alter the nature of his consciousness, is called a yogi. These three ways – of the fakir, the monk, and the yogi – have been developed by the great religious teachers. But, says Gurdjieff, there is also a *fourth way*, and this is the way taught by his own System. It could be called the way of the cunning man, for he is willing to adopt any method that will lead him to his goal. This involves work on all the other three bodies at once – the carriage, the horse, and the driver. To follow the fourth way, a man does not need to go into a monastery or retreat into the wilderness; he can continue to live a perfectly normal life. But he applies continual self-observation, and uses this to attempt to make himself less mechanical, less robotic.

To adopt slightly different imagery: we might say that man's total being could be compared to some vast cathedral organ; evolution has elaborated it over millions of years. Yet most of us have only the most rudimentary idea of how to play it; at best we can produce a few scales or an uncertain rendering of 'Chopsticks'. Our major problem is to learn about the organ by observation and experiment. With enough experiment, we could eventually learn to play symphonies and concertos – the possibilities are endless. But the first step is to *grasp* its possibilities. Most of us look at it with as little comprehension as a baby looks at a motor car. As soon as we grasp those possibilities, and begin to observe and experiment, we are following the 'fourth way'.

In subsequent talks, Gurdjieff began to elaborate on the structure of the 'organ'. Man does not possess only one mind, but several – seven, in fact. What we usually call the mind is simply the intellectual mind. Next there is the emotional mind, which controls his feelings; next, the physical mind, which controls bodily movements; next, the instinctive mind which controls such functions as digestion. Each of these minds is connected with a 'centre' – the intellectual centre, the emotional centre, the 'moving' centre (controlling bodily movements), and the instinctive centre. Apart from these, there is also a sexual centre, and two higher centres – higher emotional and higher intellectual. Each of these centres works with a different kind of energy. Our problem is that we tend to use the wrong kinds of energies – for example, we may try to do intellectual work using emotional energy or emotional work using sexual energy. According to Gurdjieff, most of the centres are inclined to steal energy from the sex centre, and in return, give the sex centre useless energy with which it cannot work. The result is that we seldom experience 'true sex'. 'It is a very big thing when the sex centre works with its own energy', said Gurdjieff – a statement that D. H. Lawrence would have understood immediately.

'Work on oneself' should begin with observation of the centres; we should try to recognize them, and then to control them. The moving centre makes a convenient starting point. If we try to rub the stomach with one hand and pat the head with the other, it is easy to see that our hands want to do the same thing. But they can be trained to function separately. In fact, with a little practice, it is possible to perform quite different movements with the two hands, the two feet and the head, all at the same time. Gurdjieff's 'dances' were basically aimed at control of the 'moving centre'. They were, in effect, an attempt to de-condition, and to re-programme, the robot.

And here, of course, one encounters a basic problem. Learning to make highly complex movements with the hands and feet may give us far greater control of the moving centre; but at the end of the day, we have merely re-programmed the robot. (A Bennett disciple who had completely mastered the 'movements' told me that he now took them for granted, and that they no longer served their purpose of increasing his sense of freedom.) So new 'shocks' are required. Gurdjieff's 'System' became, in effect, a search for new shocks – which may explain why (as we shall see later) it left so many of his students with a final sense of dissatisfaction.

This brings us to one of the central questions that strikes the critical reader of *In Search of the Miraculous*. The sheer originality of Gurdjieff's System makes an enormous impact; it seems to turn most of our accepted ideas upside down. He tells Ouspensky, for example, that knowledge is material, and that is why it could not be shared out indefinitely; a certain quantity of knowledge, like a certain quantity of food, can only go so far, and if one person gets more, another gets less. He tells Ouspensky that the moon is not a dead planet, but a planet in process of birth; it is a living being that will one day become an earth, just as the earth will one day become a sun. Moreover, human beings are basically 'food for the moon'; our purpose is to produce a certain kind of psychic energy that will feed the moon. He insists that we cannot talk about consciousness because most human beings do not possess real consciousness; they are little better than machines. Man is in prison, and he can only escape if he recognizes that he *is* in prison, and that escaping requires a carefully co-ordinated plan.

It is also quite clear that he knows a great deal about the so-called 'occult'. For example, Ouspensky described to him how, in India, he had seen a fakir lying on a bed of very sharp nails, who did not receive even a scratch. Yet the man did not seem particularly 'holy'; on the contrary, he looked half asleep. Gurdjieff replied that the man was almost certainly not particularly holy. If bribed to tell how he did it, he would probably explain that he merely had to say a particular word or phrase to himself before climbing onto the bed of nails, and he would become invulnerable. According to Gurdjieff, such a man would be trained under hypnosis, and the hypnosis would somehow make him invulnerable to the nails. Later, the hypnotist would administer post-hypnotic suggestions, telling him that whenever he repeated a certain word, he would become invulnerable. Again and again, Gurdjieff demonstrated his knowledge on such matters.

Yet there are questions upon which one simply cannot take his word. Ouspensky asks, for example, whether there is life after death; Gurdjieff replies that most people possess no 'hard core' that could survive death; only hard work upon oneself could make a man capable of surviving death. Ouspensky asks about the 'astral body'; Gurdjieff replies that the astral body can only be developed through hard work. Now there are, in fact, thousands of records of so-called 'out-of-the-body experiences', in which people have found themselves apparently outside their physical bodies. This could, of course, be some odd kind of illusion – a recurrent fantasy with its cause in some control unit of the brain. But if it is not, then it is evidence that, as the occult tradition asserts, all men possess an 'astral body'. In the same way, we may feel that the idea of life after death is wishful thinking. But anyone who takes the trouble to examine the hard evidence will find that it is oddly convincing. And *if* there is anything in it, then it applies to everyone, not just to people who have acquired an 'essential self'.

In short, the reader soon begins to feel a strong suspicion that not everything Gurdjieff says should be taken at face value. The moon landings seem to have shown beyond all doubt that the moon is not an embryonic planet, but some huge chunk of dead rock, captured by our earth millions of years ago. Gurdjieff's disciples would no doubt reply that what Gurdjieff said about the moon is nevertheless true symbolically. It would surely be simpler to accept that he said many things that he knew to be untrue, and that these should be taken as another form of the 'acting' that baffled so many of his pupils. The aim was to 'shake the mind awake', and to make his pupils see the whole question of 'what to do with our lives' in a completely different light. Gurdjieff wanted them to forget anything they had imbibed at Sunday school, or from their parents, or from vague dabblings in 'occultism' or Eastern religions. He also wanted to make sure that no one could cheapen his ideas, or dilute them and make them part of the general cultural heritage. Gurdjieff had no desire to be 'intellectually OK', to be immediately accessible to readers of the highbrow Sunday newspapers. He therefore went out of his way to make his ideas deliberately inaccessible. In some ways, he was far too successful; *Beelzebub's Tales* will always have rather less readers than Hegel's *Logic*. And Gurdjieff's System will continue to repel many of the people who could most benefit from it because they find his 'cosmological' ideas too absurd to be taken seriously.

Yet in spite of the complications he introduced, Gurdjieff's ideas are basically very simple. He told Ouspensky: 'Man's possibilities are very great. You cannot conceive even a shadow of what man is capable of attaining. But nothing can be attained in sleep. In the consciousness of a sleeping man, his illusions, his 'dreams', are mixed with reality. He lives in a subjective world and he can never escape from it. And this is the reason why he can never make use of all the powers he possesses and why he lives in only a small part of himself.'

This is, in fact, Gurdjieff's starting point: the fact that man's powers are far greater than he realizes. The same observation had been made many times in earlier centuries. One of the great best sellers of the nineteenth century was *The Night Side of Nature* by Catherine Crowe, who studied the evidence for the 'supernatural' (or, as we would now say, the paranormal) – ghosts, 'phantasms of the living', clairvoyance, dreams of the future, telepathy, 'out-of-the-body experiences', poltergeists, and so on. She concluded that the evidence for such things was, in many cases, undeniable, and that at the very least, it indicated that man possesses a whole range of powers that are *unknown to himself*. Frederick Myers, one of the founder members of the Society for Psychical Research, adopted a far more scientific and systematic approach to the problems, and in his classic work *Human Personality and Its*

Survival of Bodily Death reached the same conclusion. He argued that the unusual powers of men of genius – for example, Mozart's ability to play a concerto note for note after hearing it only once – point in the same direction as the evidence for clairvoyance, telepathy, astral projection, and so on: that we possess all kinds of 'unconscious' powers that we seldom exercise. An American newspaper editor, Thomson Jay Hudson, reached the same conclusion after studying the remarkable feats of people under hypnosis, and decided that man has two 'minds', which he called the 'objective mind' and the 'subjective mind'. The objective mind is the 'everyday self' that copes with reality; the subjective mind is the 'inner self', which is usually eclipsed by the more aggressive and assertive 'everyday self', but which can emerge when the everyday self has been immobilized by hypnosis. Hudson arrived at the conclusion that when its powers are unchained, the subjective mind can literally perform miracles; he believed that the miracles of Jesus were simply the result of his unusual power of allowing his subjective mind to express itself freely.

So this notion that man's powers are far greater than he realizes is by no means new. It was the same obscure conviction that had led Ouspensky to travel in the East, and to study magic and occultism. His encounter with Gurdjieff must have been like a bucket of cold water after these studies. Gurdjieff seemed to deny all the most cherished occult traditions. His teaching returned again and again to his fundamental insight: that most men are little more than machines, 'creatures of circumstance' and slaves of the environment. Man consists of thousands of 'selves'. But every time he has to make some real mental effort, two or three of these 'selves' fuse together. And if he can continue to make tremendous efforts of will, his inner being will gradually cease to resemble a bag full of marbles; instead, there will be increasingly large chunks of glass. And each time one of these chunks is created (Gurdjieff called it 'crystallization'), man becomes increasingly capable of a *directed* effort of will, and therefore of deliberately fusing more of them together. Little by little, he can escape this dream-like 'subjective consciousness' in which most of us spend our lives. He can experience flashes of 'objective consciousness', of seeing things as they really are. As this happens, the higher emotional and higher intellectual centres begin to function (they are inoperative in 'mechanical man'), and man at last becomes capable of exercising his latent powers.

What precisely are these latent powers? We have already encountered examples of Gurdjieff's powers in the opening chapter: of how he was able to 'cure' Fritz Peters of his nervous depression by some kind of transfer of energy, and of how he was able to induce in John Bennett a state of 'higher consciousness'. In *Fragments of an Unknown Teaching*, Ouspensky tells of his own experience of Gurdjieff's 'magical' powers. Gurdjieff had told him:

> People who have an 'astral' body can communicate with one another at a distance without having recourse to ordinary physical means. For some such communications to be possible they must establish some 'connection' between them. For this purpose, when going to different places or different countries people sometimes take with them something belonging to another, especially things that have been in contact with his body and are permeated with his emanations . . . In the same way, in order to maintain a connection with a dead person, his friends used to keep objects which had belonged to him. These things leave, as it were, a *trace* behind them, something like invisible wires or threads which remain stretched out through space. These threads connect a given object with the person, living or in certain cases dead, to whom the object belonged. Men have known this from the remotest antiquity.

(This passage seems to demonstrate that Gurdjieff accepted the idea of 'life after death' without qualification.)

Gurdjieff demonstrated his own mastery of this occult tradition. On a visit to Finland with Gurdjieff and other members of the group, Ouspensky began to experience the kind of miraculous 'facts' that Gurdjieff had promised him at one of their earliest meetings. Ouspensky was fasting and practising breathing exercises. One evening, they were sitting on the floor practising certain postures, when 'the miracle began'.

> It all started with my beginning to *hear his thoughts* . . .
> Suddenly I noticed that among the words he was saying to us all, there were 'thoughts' that were intended for me. I caught one of these thoughts and replied to it, speaking aloud . . .
> Gurdjieff nodded to me and stopped speaking. There was a fairly long pause. He sat still saying nothing. After a while I

heard his voice inside me, as it were in the chest, near the heart. He put a definite question to me . . . I answered him in the affirmative . . . Z and S [other pupils] were visibly astonished at what was taking place . . . This conversation proceeded in this fashion for not less than half an hour.

Apparently there was some kind of fundamental disagreement between Gurdjieff and Ouspensky. 'The matter was concerned with certain conditions which I had either to accept or *leave the work*.' In considerable agitation, Ouspensky went for a long walk in the forest. There he saw that Gurdjieff was right; something in himself that he had considered firm and reliable did not really exist. On the other hand, he was convinced that he had found something else that *did* exist, although he felt that Gurdjieff would only laugh at him if he tried to explain it.

When he lay in bed, he heard Gurdjieff's voice inside his chest again, and was able to answer in the same way. Ouspensky is determined not to give the reader any clue to the nature of his disagreement with Gurdjieff, so the description of what happened is annoyingly vague; it seems clear that Gurdjieff was trying to drive Ouspensky into a corner, and Ouspensky was unwilling to be driven. The telepathic conversation continued the next morning at breakfast, to the bafflement of the others. And even when Ouspensky was back in St Petersburg that evening, he not only continued to converse with Gurdjieff – who was on a train going to Moscow – but also saw him.

These experiences left Ouspensky with an important conviction: that no paranormal phenomena – clairvoyance, telepathy, foreseeing the future – can be studied in an ordinary state of consciousness. They are not like electrical or chemical phenomena, which can be studied in the laboratory under test conditions. Does this mean that all the efforts of psychical researchers are a waste of time? Not quite. What Ouspensky is saying is that they are based on a misconception: that 'ordinary consciousness' is an adequate vantage point of observation for all phenomena. Ouspensky is insisting that if these 'psychic' phenomena are to be understood, then the 'observer' must begin by *altering himself*. 'There is something in the phenomena of a higher order which requires a particular emotional state *for their observation and study*. And this excludes any "properly conducted" laboratory experiments and observations.'

This observation summarizes the essence of Gurdjieff's work. Western man's concept of knowledge is built on a fundamental error: the notion that the acquisition of knowledge only requires intelligence. It requires, in fact, a kind of *action*. Consciousness needs to be put into its 'active gear'. When this happens, then man is finally awake. Later in the *Fragments*, Ouspensky describes his own brief experience of being 'awake', and it may be regarded as the climax of the book. Gurdjieff had been forcing his students to do extremely hard physical exercise, such as running at top speed for two miles, standing with extended arms for long periods, or 'marking time' (marching on the spot) at the double.

> I had gone into a room where nobody could see me, and began to mark time at the double, trying at the same time to breathe according to a particular count, that is, to inhale during a definite number of steps and exhale during a definite number. After a certain time when I had begun to tire I noticed, that is, to speak more correctly, I felt quite clearly, that my breathing was artificial and unreliable. I felt that in a very short time I would be unable to breathe in that way while continuing to mark time at the double and that ordinary normal breathing, very accelerated of course, without any count would gain the upper hand.
>
> It became more and more difficult for me to breathe and to mark time, and to observe the count of breaths and steps. I was pouring with sweat, my head began to go round, and I thought I should fall. I began to despair of obtaining results of any kind and I had almost stopped when suddenly something seemed to crack or move inside me, and my breathing went on evenly and properly at the rate I wanted it to go, but without any effort on my part, while affording me all the amount of air I needed. It was an extraordinarily pleasant sensation. I shut my eyes and continued to mark time, breathing easily and freely and feeling exactly as though strength was increasing in me and that I was getting lighter and stronger. I thought that if I could continue to run in this way for a certain time I should get still more interesting results because waves of joyful trembling had already begun to go through my body which, as I knew from previous experiments, preceded what I called the opening of the inner consciousness.
>
> But at this moment someone came into the room and I stopped.

It is interesting to observe the similarities between this account and Bennett's account (quoted in Chapter One) of his experience at Fontainebleau. Both Ouspensky and Bennett had driven themselves beyond the point at which most people would normally give up. Suddenly, the 'moving centre' took over and began to operate instinctively. Fortunately for Bennett, no one interrupted him, and he went on to the 'opening of inner consciousness'. And we observe that this 'opening' consisted of a far greater control over consciousness than we normally possess. It is also important to note that this control consisted of the use of the imagination. Bennett thought of love, horror, surprise, and so on, and his consciousness responded instantly by providing the emotion or sensation. When I normally imagine love or horror, my consciousness responds feebly, and the impression quickly vanishes. Bennett had caught a glimpse of the true potentiality of the imagination, and of the role it plays as the intermediary between the will and the body.

Ouspensky seems to have hovered on the brink of the same recognition, but was interrupted before he could grasp it. He admits that his attempt to recreate it later was a total failure. Ouspensky's desire for intellectual certainty was satisfied by Gurdjieff's teachings. But the craving for a personal miracle of transformation remained sadly unfulfilled.

Five

The Deluge and After

EVEN IN 1915, when he met Ouspensky, Gurdjieff must have realized that his plans for an institute were in danger of collapse. Fortunately, he was not the kind of person to take it to heart. Comfort and security could be far more dangerous than uncertainty – which has the advantage of keeping the mind alert. He continued his work with the various groups, but prepared to move on when the time came. The war always loomed over them. Ouspensky was particularly struck by the sight of a lorry loaded up with crutches, on its way to a military hospital – crutches for limbs that had not yet been blown off. Rival armies were responding to purely mechanical emotions of patriotism and indignation, and nothing could stop them slaughtering one another. Ouspensky's group in St Petersburg often discussed the idea of Noah's Ark – a ship that could survive the flood of coming events, and carry its builders to safety.

At this time, Gurdjieff was continuing to work in Moscow; members of Ouspensky's group occasionally went there, and returned with notes of Gurdjieff's latest lectures. The 'work' consisted basically of self-observation, based on Gurdjieff's teaching about the 'centres'. The fundamental problem was how to 'remember oneself'. Our normal state of consciousness lacks a central 'I'. When I open my eyes in the morning, things are 'seen', but it is not *I* who sees them; it is 'the machine', the robot. Ouspensky represented the concept with a convenient diagram. When I pay attention to the external world, I am like an arrow pointing outwards. When I close my eyes and sink 'into myself', my attention becomes an arrow pointing inwards. Now I try to do *both at once* – to point the 'arrow' in and out at the same time – I immediately discover that this is incredibly difficult. After a second or two, I either forget the outside world, and sink into a daydream, or forget 'myself' and become absorbed in what I am looking at. Yet, said Gurdjieff, these moments of self-remembering, when the arrow points both ways at once, are the most important of our lives. In all moments of deep happiness, we get a feeling that could be expressed: 'What, *me – here?*' I am not only aware of what is happening to me, but that it is happening to *me*. One of Gurdjieff's most basic exercises in the Moscow days was to try to look at some object – say, a watch – and at the same time to become *aware of yourself looking at it*. His pupils soon began to realize the immense difficulty of self-remembering.

It is obvious, said Gurdjieff, that there is something badly wrong with man as he exists at present. Why should we experience so much, only to forget it immediately afterwards? Half our experience rolls off us like water off a duck's back. Yet experience is *food*, whose purpose is to enable us to evolve.

Ouspensky soon found that efforts at self-remembering could be tremendously worthwhile in this respect.

> Thus, for instance, at that time I used very much to like to wander through St Petersburg at night, and to 'sense' the houses and the streets. St Petersburg is full of these strange sensations. Houses, especially old houses, were quite alive; I all but spoke to them. There was no 'imagination' in it. I did not think of anything, I simply walked along while trying to remember myself and looked about; the sensations came by themselves.

Ouspensky was experiencing the beginning of the sense of control that Bennett experienced at Fontainebleau later.

Ouspensky also has an amusing story about an unsuccessful attempt to self-remember.

> I was once walking along the Liteiny towards the Nevsky, and in spite of all my efforts I was unable to keep my attention on self-remembering. The noise, movement, everything distracted

me. Every minute I lost the thread of attention, found it again, and then lost it again. At last I felt a kind of ridiculous irritation with myself and I turned into the street on the left having firmly decided to keep my attention on the fact that *I would remember myself* at least for some time . . . I reached the Nadejdinskaya without losing the thread of attention, except, perhaps, for short moments. Then I again turned towards the Nevsky realizing that, in quiet streets, it was easier not to lose the line of thought and wishing therefore to test myself in more noisy streets. I reached the Nevsky still remembering myself, and was already beginning to experience the strange emotional state of inner peace and confidence which comes after great efforts of this kind. Just round the corner was a tobacconist's shop where they made my cigarettes. Still remembering myself I thought I would call there and order some cigarettes.

Two hours later *I woke up* in the Tavricheskaya, that is, far away . . . The sensation of awakening was extraordinarily vivid. I can almost say that I *came to*. I remembered everything at once. How I had been walking along the Nadejdinskaya, how I had been remembering myself, how I had thought about cigarettes, and how at this thought I seemed all at once to fall and disappear into a deep sleep.

At the same time, while immersed in this sleep, I had continued to perform consistent and expedient actions . . . And on the way while driving along the Tavricheskaya, I began to feel a strange uneasiness, as though I had forgotten something. *And suddenly I remembered that I had forgotten to remember myself.*

This anecdote brings out a number of important points. First, the odd sense of deep satisfaction and control – and it could almost be compared to sexual satisfaction – that accompanies self-remembering: the birth of a deeper and wider form of consciousness. Then it is worth noting that it was the thought of cigarettes that plunged him into 'sleep'. This explains why Gurdjieff felt it so important to deliberately give up certain old habits, so that the tension thereby produced acts as an 'alarm clock'. If Ouspensky had made a resolution to stop smoking, the thought of tobacco would have served as an additional 'shock' to maintain his purpose, to strengthen the weak point of the 'octave'.

Lastly, we note that the realization that he had forgotten to remember himself was literally like waking up. Gurdjieff's assertion that ordinary consciousness is a form of sleep is not intended as a figure of speech; it should be taken literally. On another occasion, Ouspensky describes how he achieved a state of self-remembering so intense that as he walked along the street, he could actually *see* that people were asleep, and see their heads wrapped in a kind of cloud of dreams. Again, this should not be taken as a figure of speech. Self-remembering seems to bring about an odd form of 'telepathy', in which consciousness becomes aware of a far wider field of reality. It seems likely that, in a sense, Ouspensky could literally see 'into their heads'.

As the winter of 1916 dragged on, it became clear to Ouspensky that their 'Ark' was not going to protect them from the chaos that surrounded them. Just after Christmas that year, the Tsarina's favourite, Rasputin, disappeared; he had prophesied that if he was killed by peasants, Russia would remain prosperous for hundreds of years; but if it was by the aristocracy, then the royal family would be doomed and no nobles would remain in Russia. He was murdered by Prince Felix Yussupov, and his body was recovered from the Neva a few weeks later.

Gurdjieff went back to Alexandropol, his home town, and telegraphed Ouspensky to join him there. Ouspensky was intrigued by this glimpse of Gurdjieff's background, and particularly by an enlarged photograph showing a younger Gurdjieff in a frock coat. From this, says Ouspensky, he deduced what Gurdjieff's profession had been at the time, but has decided to keep the secret to himself. This was, of course, the 'hypnotist' photograph (reproduced by Bennett in *Gurdjieff: Making a New World*).

Ouspensky was puzzled. Gurdjieff seemed to be working well, unperturbed by historical events. He told Ouspensky he felt things would soon quieten down and he would be able to continue his work in Russia. (If he was serious – which is something one can never be sure about with Gurdjieff – he was being singularly short-sighted.) Yet Gurdjieff was obviously brooding. On what? Probably on the feeling that his 'method' was still unsatisfactory, and that something new was needed – something more *practical*. People can comfortably absorb new ideas and go back to sleep. He had to devise new methods of keeping them awake.

Ouspensky returned to St Petersburg. Gurdjieff told him

that he proposed to go to Kislovodsk to set up a new work group, and advised Ouspensky – and anyone else who was interested – to join him there. In fact, Gurdjieff went to Essentuki, in the Caucasus. He rented a villa, and a house on the edge of the village; there, for six weeks, his pupils worked with a new kind of intensity. To begin with, Gurdjieff introduced various exercises and techniques. Some of the exercises involved muscular exertion or relaxation, and would be familiar to any yoga student of today. Others were more complex. It was here that Gurdjieff introduced one of his most startling and spectacular exercises: the 'stop' exercise. When he called 'stop', everyone had to stop *instantaneously* whatever they were doing, even if they were halfway through a step, or swallowing a mouthful of food. It was, he said, to try to make people aware of their way of doing things, of their exact posture and muscular response. In later years at the Prieuré, he might walk into the dormitory in the middle of the night and snap his fingers, and everyone had to be out of bed and in some complicated posture within a matter of seconds. He was trying to cultivate total *alertness*.

Gurdjieff explained that he was introducing them to the principle of super-effort. If a man walks twenty-five miles in bad weather, and gets home cold and hungry – and then decides to walk another two miles before going indoors, that is super-effort.

Here, I feel, Gurdjieff was failing to explain something important. It is not the super-effort itself that is important, but the energy we *summon* to meet it. The whole point of Gurdjieff's 'system' – and this is never sufficiently emphasized either in his own books or in those about him – is its basic assumption that man possesses far more energy than he realizes – a vast lake of 'vital reserves'. What cuts us off from these reserves is a feeling of laziness, or rather, of *reluctance*. We contemplate some effort, and think: 'What a bore.' And this feeling of boredom instantly lowers our vitality. If I performed a super-effort – like walking the additional two miles – with a groan of self-pity, it would be completely useless. Yet if some sudden crisis – or some sudden piece of good news (i.e. someone I love is waiting for me two miles away) – made me decide to walk the two miles, I would do it with a springy step, prepared, if necessary, to go ten times as far. This, then, is the real aim of the exercise: to summon that state of optimism, of inner purpose, that makes the super-effort easy. As the story of Fritz Peters demonstrates (see Chapter 1), Gurdjieff had mastered the trick of drawing on these vital reserves, overruling his 'reluctance'.

But the practical significance of Gurdjieff's doctrine of super-effort was that he felt it provided a new basis for the 'work'. In St Petersburg or Moscow, the 'work' had been purely internal, so to speak. Now Gurdjieff was quite deliberately looking for difficulties to which he could subject his followers, with the deliberate aim of making them 'summon' the necessary energy and attention. For example, when his pupil Thomas de Hartmann – an ex-army officer – arrived with his wife, Gurdjieff called to a follower called Zaharoff to make tea in a samovar. This involved a difficult ritual of lighting tiny pieces of wood and coal under the samovar; they burned only with difficulty, and if Zaharoff turned away for a moment, they went out, and he had to start all over again. For the remainder of his life, Gurdjieff apparently took immense pleasure in causing trouble and confusion – at one period, Fritz Peters broke with him in a rage. The aim was to force his pupils to make 'super-efforts'. Gurdjieff took Hartmann and his wife into the village to buy cake, and on the way back, accelerated his pace until they were practically running; again, it was an effort to accustom his pupils to super-effort.

Thomas de Hartmann's book, *Our Life with Mr Gurdjieff*, is perhaps one of the most fascinating and revealing of all accounts of Gurdjieff as a person. He goes on to recount another of Gurdjieff's deliberate 'tricks'. At Essentuki, he announced he intended to go to Persia – creating immediate alarm and confusion among his followers. Hartmann, for one, was still an officer, and could not become a deserter without much agony of conscience. But on the day announced for his departure, Gurdjieff declared he was only going to go to Tuapse, close to the Black Sea, and said that anyone who wanted to come was welcome. The Hartmanns and several others decided to go. But at Tuapse, they found Gurdjieff lying in bed, apparently in a state of indecision. There was a 'heavy atmosphere which overwhelms one when he does not know what to do.' And Hartmann adds penetratingly: 'Mr Gurdjieff certainly knew how to create such an atmosphere.' In other words, Gurdjieff realized that his followers were now becoming dependent on his own strong sense of purpose, and wanted to try and shake them out of this habit before it had time to consolidate.

What followed is again typical. Gurdjieff bought a cart and announced that they would now leave. Gurdjieff drove off with the cart and luggage, and told the Hartmanns to walk over the mountains and meet him some miles away. The walk was long, hard and hot, and they finally discovered an inn where they could wait. Finally, after dark, Gurdjieff arrived. But instead of letting them go to bed, he proposed to continue the journey by moonlight. They plodded on – Madame de Hartmann in high-heeled shoes – until two in the morning, when it began to rain; Gurdjieff told them to make a fire, then said they would sleep – all except Hartmann, who was ordered to sit up on guard duty.

The next day, Hartmann was dizzy with fatigue, and Gurdjieff told him to climb on to the luggage on the cart. But Hartmann discovered that if he closed his eyes, he fell off the cart; so he had to fight against sleep. This, of course, is precisely what Gurdjieff intended. He believed that, through intense efforts, a certain form of energy is created – the energy man needs for self-transformation. Without that energy, he can think about self-transformation, even long for it, but can never achieve it.

And so the journey went on. At least Hartmann realized the purpose behind it. 'By speaking of going to Persia and by creating all kinds of emotional and physical difficulties, he was creating in strange surroundings a ladder of obstacles over which we had to pass to reach a certain little *do* in ourselves – the *do* in the scale of our general development.'

In a place called Outch-Dary, Hartmann became seriously ill, after eating plums from a tree (against Gurdjieff's advice), and came close to death. In his delirium, he even tried to kill his wife. When Gurdjieff came in, Hartmann hurled himself at him in a frenzy. But when Gurdjieff placed his hand on his forehead he felt a deep sense of peace, and relaxed. Gurdjieff still possessed his 'magical' powers. Eventually, Hartmann recovered, and they returned to Essentuki. The journey had apparently been designed to place the Hartmanns under unusual stress.

The same applied to an amusing incident involving a restaurant. Hartmann felt that he would like to go to a social club and Gurdjieff pretended to think that he and a doctor friend were invited for supper. Inflation was a serious problem and Hartmann had no regular income; nevertheless, he took them to the restaurant. Gurdjieff proceeded to order the most expensive meal available, and Hartmann had to tip the waiter to go to his wife and collect another 500 roubles. But the next day, Gurdjieff returned the money to Hartmann, explaining that it had been done for his own good. Hartmann was still not behaving like an adult – as his misery and embarrassment about the meal demonstrated. It was the juvenile part of him that was being made to squirm.

The situation in Russia was now serious. The Bolshevik revolution had taken place; the provisional Kerensky government had been overthrown; Russia was torn by civil war. Students like Hartmann – and other ex-officers – were in danger. But for the moment, the Bolsheviks had only advanced as far as the northern slopes of the Caucasus; to the south, the Mensheviks – moderate socialists who opposed Bolshevism – were still in power. Unfortunately, Gurdjieff and his students were in Bolshevik territory. Gurdjieff began by ensuring good relations with the local Bolsheviks; he told one of his students, a White Russian lawyer, to go and offer his legal services to them. The lawyer managed to convince them that he was an ardent revolutionary, by making a fiery speech about Proudhon and Fourier, and was instantly accepted.

Gurdjieff also told the lawyer to write to the Essentuki Soviet, making a formal request to organize a scientific expedition to Mount Induc in the Caucasus; they would, he explained, search for standing stones – dolmens – and also for gold. Gurdjieff cunningly arranged for an article to appear in a newspaper in Piatigorsk – headquarters of the higher Soviet for the region – describing the expedition and the importance of its aims. Permission was given. Gurdjieff even persuaded the Bolsheviks to supply quantities of pure alcohol for 'washing the gold'; it was diluted for their own consumption. (Alcohol of any kind was by then unobtainable.) The lawyer, who was by now in charge of the passport office, issued them all with Soviet passports.

Hartmann was puzzled to see Gurdjieff beating the horses on the belly and making them rear up in anger and alarm. He understood why when soldiers later came to requisition the horses, then brought them back two hours later, declaring that they were dangerous. Finally, the Bolsheviks provided the 'expedition' with a train to take them to Maikop, on the edge of Bolshevik territory. Two weeks after they had left Essentuki, a reign of terror began, and all ex-officers were shot.

Maikop fell into the hands of White Russian forces; it became necessary to obtain more passports, and the White Russians were difficult. But Gurdjieff's luck held; an admiral who was an old friend of one of the group appeared, and arranged everything. The day after Gurdjieff and his party left Maikop, it was retaken by the Bolsheviks. But by then they were on their way south. The journey to Tiflis was difficult and dangerous; at one point, Hartmann and his party were held up and robbed by brigands. (Gurdjieff – with typical luck – had gone ahead at this point and experienced no difficulties.) Fortunately, Hartmann's wife persuaded them out of taking some of their essential supplies. They were lucky to escape unscathed; other travellers had been killed on the same road.

Gurdjieff's announced intention of seeking for standing stones was not pure fiction. When, in a mountain village, he heard that there were dolmens in the area, he asked to be taken to one. The dolmen in question proved to be a sort of giant stone coffer with a lid. Asked about the nature of such stones, Gurdjieff replied that they were 'road signs' showing the way to places of initiation – a view that reveals that he possessed some esoteric knowledge about the stones and the purpose. This is confirmed by what happened next. Gurdjieff asked their guides if there were any more dolmens in the area; they said no. He then made certain measurements and calculations, and led them through thick woods, which had to be cleared with hand axes. He led the party to two more dolmens, both heavily overgrown and unknown to local people. Their guides were astonished. In his own account of the journey, Gurdjieff has the cryptic remark that various experts among his pupils – in engineering, astronomy, archaeology – helped him to 'resolve the problem of the dolmens'. It is a pity that no record seems to exist of his 'solution'.

Finally, they arrived in Tiflis, the capital of Georgia, still in Menshevik hands. Gurdjieff not only had his followers to support, but also twenty-eight relatives, who had left Alexandropol in the face of the advancing Turks. (Gurdjieff's father had been killed.) Gurdjieff was himself still suffering from an illness he had contracted during the journey; but with typical determination, he set out to make money. Some of his students were sent to the surrounding area to buy up old carpets at rag-and-bone prices; others washed and repaired them; then the carpets were sold. In a few weeks, the business was flourishing and they had more than enough money for all their needs. It was another example of Gurdjieff's basic assertion: that those who are good at 'the work' would also be good at the practical business of staying alive.

In Tiflis, Gurdjieff once again set up his institute, with a certain amount of help from the government. He was slowly refining and developing his 'method'. Before leaving Essentuki, he had introduced the 'movements' or sacred dances as a basic discipline of the 'moving centre' – the aim was to endow the body with its own form of 'consciousness'. Now he produced a prospectus in which he spoke of 'Exercises for the development of will, memory, attention, hearing, thinking, emotion, instinct.' But the situation was precarious. The Georgian government was propped up by a British military presence; and when the British decided to withdraw, it was only a matter of time before the Bolsheviks took over.

The head of British military intelligence in Constantinople was a young British officer named John Bennett. Like Gurdjieff, he was fascinated by the dervishes and their ceremonies. He had seen an old dervish lying on his back, with a razor sharp sword across his body, and a man standing on the sword; yet the old dervish's body was not even marked. Bennett had become convinced that the answer to the mystery of our human limitations lies in the concept of the fifth dimension.

Bennett had already met Ouspensky in Constantinople. Ouspensky had, by this time, decided to separate from Gurdjieff. The reason he gives – in *In Search of the Miraculous* – is that he felt Gurdjieff's work was becoming increasingly oriented towards religion. The real reason, almost certainly, is that Ouspensky was too dominant and original a mind to remain anyone's 'disciple', and that he found Gurdjieff's enigmatic personality too devious and oriental for his westernized comprehension. In Constantinople they pursued their separate ways. Ouspensky's first book *Tertium Organum* had recently been translated into English, and become something of a best seller – it led to Ouspensky being invited to London by Lady Rothermere. Bennett was not impressed by Ouspensky's ideas. And when he heard of Gurdjieff's presence in Constantinople, his first reaction was suspicion; he had received a despatch warning him that Gurdjieff was a Bolshevik agent.

His first meeting with Gurdjieff dispelled all doubts. This man 'with the strangest eyes I had ever seen' obviously possessed a vast and precise knowledge of subjects that Bennett only knew as a beginner. Bennett was invited to watch Gurdjieff's students perform their sacred 'movements', and was deeply impressed. It was a fascination that was to last a lifetime.

For a year – until September 1921 – Gurdjieff ran his institute from Constantinople. He had also – oddly enough – set up as a psychiatrist, and it was in this capacity that he cured a young Greek of drug addiction and alcoholism. In return, he had been given a half share in a ship, which had been requisitioned by the British navy. With Bennett's help, Gurdjieff was able to get the ship released and sold; his half-share provided enough money to realize an ambition he had felt ever since landing in Constantinople: to move his institute to Europe.

Six

The Awakening of Courage

You think you know who you are and what you are; but you do not know either what slaves you now are, or how free you might become. Man can do nothing: he is a machine controlled by external influences, not by his own will, which is an illusion. He is asleep. He has no permanent self that he can call 'I'. Because he is not one but many; his moods, his impulses, his very sense of his own existence are no more than a constant flux. You need not believe what I tell you, but if you will observe yourselves you will verify its truth. Make the experiment of trying to remember your own existence and you will find that you cannot remember yourselves even for two minutes. How can man, who cannot remember who and what he is, who does not know the forces that move him to action, pretend that he can do anything? No, the first truth that must be grasped is that you and I and all men are nothing but machines. Man has no power to direct his private affairs, and he is equally helpless in his social and political life.*

This was the doctrine that Ouspensky taught in a London flat at 38 Warwick Gardens, in 1922. One indignant listener, the 'occultist', A. E. Waite, stood up and said 'Mr Ouspensky, there is no love in your system', and walked out of the room. But he was the exception. The rest of Ouspensky's audiences – which included many professional doctors, psychiatrists

Witness, J. G. Bennett, p 87.

and writers – found his doctrines startling, original and fascinating.

As a Russian exile, Ouspensky was lucky to get a foothold in London. Gurdjieff also attempted to set up his Institute in Hampstead, but was unable to obtain the necessary visas. It made no difference; he had already decided that Paris would be more suitable. (An earlier plan to establish himself in Germany was dropped when he realized that the political situation there was as volatile as in Russia or Turkey.)

Before leaving London, Gurdjieff gave a number of remarkable lectures. Bennett was present at some of these and took notes, which he quotes in *Gurdjieff, Making a New World*. Again, they reveal the remarkable *scientific* precision of Gurdjieff's insights. Gurdjieff was speaking of one of his most fundamental concepts: the difference between 'personality' and 'essence'. When a baby is born, it has only 'essence', its essential response to the world. At the age of six or seven the child begins to develop 'personality' – that is, to become aware of itself as a person among other people – *in response* to other people. And when this happens, says Gurdjieff, 'essence' often ceases to grow altogether; personality takes over. Some people who appear to have a powerful and vital personality are really empty inside; their essence ceased to develop as a child.

In *In Search of the Miraculous*, Ouspensky describes an extraordinary experiment performed by Gurdjieff to show his pupils the difference between essence and personality. Two people had been chosen for the purpose of the experiment; one a prominent middle-aged man with an important position, the other a rather scatter-brained young man whose conversation tended to be wordy and confusing. In some way, either by hypnosis or a drug (Ouspensky declined to be specific), both were plunged into a semi-trance-like state in which 'personality' vanished.* The older man became completely passive. Asked about the war – about which he had been expressing the most heated opinions a moment before – he said that it did not interest him. The young man, on the other hand, talked seriously and simply, making excellent sense. Gurdjieff explained that the young man had a reason-

---

*In *Venture With Ideas*, Kenneth Walker says that Ouspensky told him Gurdjieff used a drug on this occasion.

ably developed 'essence' which had become overlaid with awkwardness, a tendency to overreact to other people, so he appeared a nervous fool. The older man had little 'essence' left; he had developed a bombastic and opinionated personality, but there was nothing underneath.

At the end of the London lectures, Gurdjieff developed this concept of essence and personality: 'What you call "will" in yourself is only from personality. It has no connection with real will. Something touches personality and it says "I want" or "I do not want" . . . and thinks it is will. It is nothing. It is passive. Will can be only in essence.'

Essence, Gurdjieff explained, *has no critical mind*:

> It is trustful, but because it does not know, it is apprehensive. You cannot influence essence by logical argument, or convince it. Until essence begins to experience for itself, it remains as it always was. Sometimes situations arise where personality cannot react, and essence has to react. Then it is seen how much there is in [a person's] essence. Perhaps it is only a child and does not know how to behave. It is no use telling it to behave differently, because it will not understand your language.

Perhaps the most significant statement in this lecture on essence and personality is the following: 'Essence and personality are even in different parts of the brain.' At the time he made this statement, it could have meant very little even to the doctors and psychologists in his audience – unless they happen to recall a tag of the neurologist Hughlings Jackson, who remarked: 'Expression on the left, recognition on the right.' What he meant was that the human brain seems to be divided into two parts, and the left cerebral hemisphere is concerned with language and logic, while the right is concerned with recognition (i.e. of faces) and intuition. It was not until well after the death of Gurdjieff that an American scientist, R. W. Sperry, tried the experiment of cutting the isthmus of nerve fibre joining the two halves of the brain, and made the astonishing discovery that we literally have *two different persons* inside our heads. If a 'divided brain' patient is shown something with his left eye only (which is connected, for some odd reason, to the right side of the brain), and asked what he has been shown, he cannot reply. But if he is asked to write what he has seen with his left hand, he can write its name without any trouble. If he is shown an orange with his left eye and an apple with his right, and he is asked what he has just seen, he replies: 'An apple'. Asked to write down what he has seen with the left hand, he writes: 'An orange'. Asked what he has just written, he replies: 'An apple'. If he is shown an indecent picture with the left eye only, he will blush. Asked why he is blushing, he replies truthfully: 'I don't know.'

That is to say, the 'I' inhabits the left side of the brain, the side connected with language and logic. A few centimetres away there is another 'I', an 'I' without a voice, of which the left appears to be totally unaware.

Psychologists are still completely ignorant of the nature of hypnosis. How is it that a person can be placed in a trance, and then persuaded to do things that he could not do in his conscious state: stop smoking, make warts disappear, even lie rigid between two chairs while a heavy man stands on his stomach? In trance, the conscious ego falls asleep, while some part of one's inner being remains wide awake. (A hypnotized person's brain rhythms are the same as when he is wide awake.) This suggests that hypnosis causes the left-brain to fall asleep, while the right remains awake. And when the critical, conscious ego is asleep, our natural powers can express themselves without constrictions. (We all know how too much self-consciousness makes us clumsy and inefficient.)

Anyone can learn a great deal about these two 'selves' by ordinary self-observation. For example, it is clear that the left-brain is the source of all ordinary acts of will: 'I' decide to do something. But the right-brain seems to be responsible for our *energy supplies*. When 'I' become tired and jaded, I can quickly renew myself if I can forget the ego, become deeply absorbed in something that 'takes me out of myself'. This is clearly a trick that Gurdjieff understood, and which explains how he was able to renew his energies so quickly after 'recharging' the exhausted Fritz Peters.

In short, self-observation seems to confirm that we consist of two different 'selves' and that these correspond to Gurdjieff's essence and personality. What is most amazing is that Gurdjieff knew they could be located in different parts of the brain, although it seems likely that he knew nothing of brain physiology. Again, we are forced to conclude that he may have been telling the truth when he claimed that his system was based upon some ancient scientific knowledge that had been long forgotten by most of the human race.

In France, Gurdjieff soon located a house that seemed to be ideal for the setting up of his institute: the Chateau du Prieuré, near Fontainebleau, formerly the home of Madame de Maintenon, second wife of Louis the Fourteenth. It had large and rambling grounds – providing plenty of opportunity for 'work'. Gurdjieff rented it for a year, with an option to buy. But it left him penniless. Again, he had to find ways to make large sums of money. He started two Paris restaurants, and entered the oil business; he also set up once again as a psychiatrist, offering to cure alcoholism and drug addiction. His success in this field was apparently remarkable, although at present we possess no published account of his methods. All this involved enormous overwork, and the stretching of his vital energies to their limits. He tells us, driving back to the Prieuré one night in a state of exhaustion, he fell asleep, but somehow stopped the car at the side of the road; he was awakened next morning by a farm wagon trying to get past. As a result, he caught a severe chill whose effects were long-lasting.

One student, Gladys Alexander, wrote:

Life [at the Prieuré] was spurred to a highly accelerated pace. It ranged from the heavy toil of the old-fashioned kitchen and scullery, from the work of the house and the laundry, the flower and kitchen gardens, to the care of horses, donkey cart, sheep and goats, cows and calves, hens, pigs, and dogs. It was lived in a seething atmosphere of speed and tension, of zeal and high hopes.

It was Gurdjieff's friend Pogossian who had told him the basic secret about work. Pogossian never relaxed; he always moved his arms rhythmically, marked time with his feet; he explained that his aim was to accustom his nature to love work, to overcome its natural laziness. Now Gurdjieff applied the lesson to his pupils.

But this was not the only purpose of the physical hard work at the Prieuré. It also sprang from Gurdjieff's recognition that 'personality' is one of the major obstacles to self-actualization. Personality is a fool; it over-reacts, it distrusts itself, it is inclined to despair. We can see this in the case of the young man whose 'essence' was far more sensible and controlled than his personality, which behaved like a buffoon. The problem becomes twice as difficult if there is a lack of serious aim and objective. Hard work and serious aims soon teach the personality to shut up and keep quiet. Many of Gurdjieff's pupils were rich people who had never done a hard day's work in their lives. So hard work was an essential first step in readjusting their inner balance. Physical labour has another immense advantage. When the body is tired, it relaxes; the 'personality' takes the hint, and also makes itself inconspicuous. This explains, for example, why it is far easier to 'sink into' music or poetry when you are physically tired. The personality ceases to form an obstacle, a barrier. It ceases to chatter and interrupt. So the contact between the essence of the listener and the essence of the music – or poetry – is more immediate and direct. And the contact between Gurdjieff's essence and that of his pupils would also become more direct.

Predictably, there was a great deal of misunderstanding and criticism. Rom Landau says in *God Is My Adventure* (published in 1935), 'Some of the pupils would at times complain that they could no longer support Gurdjieff's violent temper, his apparent greed for money, or the extravagance of his private life.' The last is probably intended as a covert reference to Gurdjieff's reputation for seducing his female students. (In Providence, Rhode Island, in 1960, a man was pointed out to me as one of Gurdjieff's illegitimate children. The professor who told me this also assured me that Gurdjieff had left many children around America.)* A consumptive Russian girl, Irene Reweliotty, who was introduced to the 'work' by her lover Luc Dietrich, was invited to dinner by Gurdjieff, who asked her (in Russian) to return after the other guests had left. Convinced that he had seduction in mind, she telephoned to say that her mother was expecting her home. 'Gurdjieff then insulted her in a way that left her no doubt of his intentions,' says Louis Pauwels in his book on Gurdjieff. When she told another disciple about this, he slapped her face. A few days later, she died of a heart attack.

*[Gurdjieff] spoke of women in terms that would have better suited a fanatical Muslim polygamist than a Christian, boasting that he had many children by different women, and that women were for him only the means to an end.' – *Witness*, J. G. Bennett, p 258.

But the accusation most frequently brought against Gurdjieff was that he reduced his pupils to automata through overwork. One woman disciple vomited blood and the doctor diagnosed a burst ulcer; Gurdjieff denied that it was blood and offered a different diagnosis. But an operation was to reveal that the doctor had been correct. The impression that Gurdjieff treated his students like a brutal drill sergeant was strengthened by stories that were circulated after the death of Katherine Mansfield. The New Zealand writer was already dying of tuberculosis when she decided to ask Gurdjieff if she could come to the Prieuré in October 1922. For the first six weeks she was allowed to live as an onlooker, then expected to join in with the work, preparing meals in the kitchen. Gurdjieff decided that she needed the breath of cows to improve her health, and actually installed a couch above the cows in the barn, where she could sit and inhale. It was all to no avail, and in January, ten weeks after her arrival, she died of a haemorrhage. Her letters to her husband, Middleton Murry, make it clear that there was no attempt to overwork her. But her death gave Gurdjieff's Institute a sinister reputation.

All the same, it is clear that the hard work *could* be dangerous. Bennett not only survived his attacks of dysentery and overwork, but gained from them. Those with weaker spirits or less persistence may well have collapsed from exhaustion. Louis Pauwels states that 'after two years of "work" ... I found myself in hospital, as weak as a kitten, one eye nearly gone, on the verge of suicide and calling desperately for help at 3 o'clock in the morning.' And he speaks of two American girls who had spent two years in a group directed by Madame de S. (presumably Jeanne de Salzmann): 'They were at their last gasp, ready to take the plunge into death, in fact, already bending over it – fascinated.' He advised them to break away from the 'teaching' and retire to a seaside resort.

All of which brings us to the heart of the Gurdjieff problem. As a young man – as we have seen – Gurdjieff was driven half frantic by the sense of his inability to control his 'forgetfulness'. For *this* is the central human problem: ordinary forgetfulness, like walking into a room to get something, and forgetting what you went in for. When we get something we want badly, or experience some enormous relief from misery or crisis, we feel that *we shall never forget* this happiness; but twenty-four hours later, nothing but a dim carbon copy remains, and we are again wholly absorbed in trivialities. If we could take a course in *not* 'forgetting', our lives would obviously be completely transformed. And, after all, any intelligent person can train himself to be less absent-minded. It seems preposterous that nothing except a little absent-mindedness stands between us and a life that is ten times as satisfying as the present one. Anybody who realizes this experiences Gurdjieff's tremendous sense of frustration, and is willing to make the most exhausting efforts to 'break through'.

And therein lies the problem. For exhaustion makes things ten times as bad. When we are healthy and wide awake we are always experiencing the sudden flash of sheer 'absurd delight' that reawakens our sense of meaning and purpose. But exhaustion makes everything seem dead, so that no effort seems worth making. The world becomes 'stale, flat and unprofitable'. And if we are *taken in* by this apparent meaninglessness, this is a highly dangerous state. It becomes a vicious circle of depression and fatigue. Without a sense of purpose, a human being is like a sailor without a compass.

For men like Ouspensky and Bennett, the danger did not exist. Long before they met Gurdjieff, they had spent years searching for some kind of knowledge; so no amount of fatigue was likely to make them lose heart – that is, to be *taken in* by the sense of meaninglessness. A person like Katherine Mansfield was a different proposition. Even John Carswell's sympathetic book about her* makes it clear that she was an emotional dilettante, driven by a mixture of egoism and boredom. If she had recovered her health at the Prieuré, she might well have gone off and written a satirical short story about it all, portraying Gurdjieff as a charlatan. Gurdjieff was subjected to a great deal of criticism for the manner in which he got rid of unsatisfactory pupils – like Zaharoff, whom he sent back to Petrograd from Essentuki – but it seems clear that he failed to exercise enough of this kind of selectivity.

What emerges clearly from Gurdjieff's own account of the founding of Fontainebleau Institute is that he was in a state of physical exhaustion for much of the time, and was permanently

---

Life and Letters – Studies of A. R. Orage, Beatrice Hastings, Katherine Mansfield, J. M. Murry and S. S. Koteliansky. London 1978. Carswell's account of Gurdjieff is unsympathetic and ill-informed, but should be read as an interesting example of the kind of misunderstanding Gurdjieff continues to arouse.

worried about money. If he drove his pupils to the limits of endurance, he also drove himself. And, as Bennett acknowledges, it worked.

> In spite of the obstacles, Gurdjieff during the period from November 1922 to December 1923 had accomplished something that had never been seen in Europe before. He created conditions for work that enabled scores of people to verify for themselves the potential for transformation that is latent in every human being. The basic method was simple: it consisted of offering pupils the opportunity and the means of stretching to the limit the capacity of their physical body for work, for attention, for the acquisition of skills, and for the production of psychic energy . . . No description of the external life at the Prieuré can give any adequate idea of what was happening inside people. They could see for themselves that miracles were possible and were occurring before their eyes. The atmosphere was happy and vital, not gloomy and monastic.

But to emphasize the work itself would be to miss the whole point. In a basic sense, the work was totally unimportant. Two stories illustrate this. Bennett says that one day Gurdjieff announced that ordinary physical labour was not enough: they all had to learn various skills: shoe-making, engineering, basket-weaving, and so on. He asked for volunteers, and everybody raised his hand. But the actual instruction failed to materialize. However, Bennett makes the interesting remark that the *expectation* of all this additional work galvanized everybody and made them more energetic.

Fritz Peters was told to mow the lawns once every four days. When he had achieved this, Gurdjieff – instead of praising him – told him that he now had to do it all in one day. Seeing Peter's disappointment and frustration, he took him to a nearby field, full of high grass, and told him when he had learned to mow the lawns in one day, he would be transferred to this field, which he would have to learn to scythe in one day. (Peters was a rather small eleven-year-old at the time.) Understandably, Peter's heart sank at the prospect. Yet he pressed on and managed to mow all the lawns in one day, finding that his self-pity and resentment vanished as he worked. When, finally, he asked Gurdjieff when he had to scythe the field, Gurdjieff made the curious reply: 'Not necessary. You have already done the work.' That is to say, the prospect of the far harder job of scything the field had made Peters begin to treat his lawn-mowing problem as a minor task. *This* is what Gurdjieff was interested in – something that might be called 'the awakening of courage'.

In early 1924, Gurdjieff's precarious financial position made him decide to try to refill his coffers in America. A demonstration of his dances at the Théâtre des Champs-Elysées in December 1923 was a considerable success, and it may have been this that gave Gurdjieff the idea of earning money across the Atlantic. Ouspensky was able to help by putting him in contact with Claude Bragdon, who had translated *Tertium Organum*. A. R. Orage, who had given up the editorship of the *New Age* to work with Gurdjieff, was sent ahead to prepare the ground. (Orage ended by staying on in New York.) Gurdjieff and his troupe arrived in January 1924 – forty of them – and gave a demonstration at Leslie's Ballroom on the 23rd.

The pupils performed their 'movements', to the accompaniment of eastern music and a beating drum, and then gave an exhibition of 'magnetism, clairvoyance and mind-reading'. Members of the audience were asked to show some personal object to a pupil in the audience. Pupils on stage then gave accurate descriptions of what had been shown. Names of operas were suggested to pupils in the audience, who 'transferred' the information to Thomas de Hartmann on stage, who then played excerpts from the opera. In the same way, pupils in the audience 'transmitted' the names of living animals to an artist on stage, who then drew them on large sheets of white paper. It was a remarkable exhibition of mind-reading, and at least one member of the audience, A. S. Nott (who later wrote *Teachings of Gurdjieff: The Journal of a Pupil*), was baffled and deeply impressed. Another member, William Seabrook, was inclined to dismiss them as mere conjuring tricks. (Orage told the audience that the performance would involve 'tricks, half-tricks and true supernatural phenomena', and left the audience to guess which was which.) Seabrook wrote:

> What excited and interested me was the amazing, brilliant, automaton-like, inhuman, almost incredible docility and robot-like obedience of the disciples. They were like a group of perfectly trained zombies, or like circus animals . . .
> The group consisted of young and youngish women, most

of whom were handsome and some of whom were beautiful; and of men who looked as if they had come, and probably did in most cases, from the best British and Continental homes and universities. I met some of these disciples, and they were almost without exception people of culture, breeding and intelligence ... And there was no fake about it, regardless of whether it was supernormal or not, because if they hadn't learned supreme co-ordination, they'd have broken their arms and legs, and maybe their necks, in some of the stunts they did. But what I felt the demonstrations showed, even more than their control over themselves, was the terrific domination of Gurdjieff, the Master. At his command, they'd race, spread out, at breakneck speed, from left to right across the stage, and at another low command from him, freeze full flight as if caught by a race-track camera ...

Gurdjieff himself, a calm, bull-like man, with muscles in those days hard as steel, in immaculate dinner clothes, his head shaven like a Prussian officer's, with black luxuriant handle-bar moustaches, and generally smoking expensive Egyptian cigarettes, stood casually down in the audience, or off to one side beside the piano ... He never shouted. He was always casual. Yet always in complete command. It was as if he were a slave-master or wild-animal tamer, with an invisible bull-whip slashing inaudibly through the air. Among his other qualities, he was a great showman, and a climax came one night which literally had the front row out of their seats. The troupe was deployed extreme back stage, facing the audience. At his command, they came racing full tilt towards the footlights. We expected to see a wonderful exhibition of arrested motion. But instead, Gurdjieff calmly turned his back, and was lighting a cigarette. In the next split second, an aerial human avalanche was flying through the air, across the orchestra, down among empty chairs, on the floor, bodies pell-mell, piled on top of each other, arms and legs sticking out in weird postures – frozen there, fallen, in complete immobility and silence.

Only after it had happened did Gurdjieff turn and look at them, as they lay there, still immobile. When they presently arose, by his permission, and it was evident that no arms, legs or necks had been broken – no one seemed to have suffered even so much as a scratch or bruise – there were storms of applause, mingled with a little protest. It had been almost too much.*

*William Seabrook: *Witchcraft, Its Power in the World Today* (1942), Part 2, Chapter 3.

Llewellyn Powys also has a brief description of the Gurdjieff troupe in *The Verdict of Bridlegoose*:

> [Gurdjieff] had a high, bald head, with sharp, black eyes. His general appearance made one think of a riding master, though there was something about his presence that affected one's nerves in a strange way. Especially did one feel this when his pupils came on to the stage, to perform like a hutchful of hypnotized rabbits under the gaze of a master conjurer.*

In spite of much favourable publicity, the New York audiences steadily diminished. In the midst of the jazz age, New Yorkers were not deeply interested in oriental dances. The 'troupe' was actually looking for other work when Adolf Bolm, late of the Diaghilev ballet, invited them to Chicago. Their performances there were a success, as was a final performance at Carnegie Hall. But the American visit had not brought Gurdjieff as much as he had hoped.

Olga de Hartmann has a typical story of Gurdjieff at this period. He asked her to return to Paris alone, because he needed her husband with him in New York for a while. She flatly refused; Gurdjieff was displeased, but knew she was immovable. She and her husband returned to Paris without Gurdjieff. When she had purchased the boat tickets, she realized they had no money left, so she pawned one of her rings. It was one she particularly valued, and she left a message for her brother – who was in New York – to redeem it. In fact, Gurdjieff found out about it, and redeemed it himself, giving it back to her when he returned to the Prieuré. He was not a man to bear grudges.

Back at Fontainebleau, work continued as usual. On 5 July 1924, Gurdjieff spent the day in Paris. The steering wheel of his car needed attention, and he left it at a garage. He told Olga de Hartmann to do some secretarial work at his Paris flat, then return to the Prieuré by train. She was annoyed because it was a hot day, and she usually drove back with Gurdjieff in the car. In Gurdjieff's flat she fell asleep and was suddenly awakened by his voice calling to her. But he was nowhere to be seen.

In fact, Gurdjieff had crashed into a tree – probably due to

The Verdict of Bridlegoose, Chapter 17.

the defective steering column – and was lying badly injured and unconscious at the time she heard his voice.

Seven

New Directions

GURDJIEFF'S accident – which brought him close to death – was the beginning of a new epoch in his life. He decided that his ideas had to be transmitted to posterity. One morning, in the Café de la Paix, he started dictating to Olga de Hartmann: 'It was in the year 223 after the creation of the World . . . Through the Universe flew the ship *Karnak* of the 'trans-space' communication'. It was the beginning of his enormous book *Beelzebub's Tales to His Grandson*.

This was a period of deep gloom for everybody. Gurdjieff's accident left the disciples shattered; they felt he should be invulnerable. Gurdjieff himself was profoundly shaken; he felt that the accident had caused his consciousness to revert to an earlier stage in its development. In his state of broken physical health, it was obvious that the institute could not continue in the same way as before. He announced to his assembled students that he intended to close it down. Most of the Russians packed up and left the following day. In fact, the institute continued to function. But Gurdjieff no longer looked upon it as his life's work.

There were further problems. His mother – who, together with his sister and brother, was living at the Prieuré – was suffering from a liver complaint; soon after his accident, she died. Gurdjieff had been deeply attached to her, and it was a considerable blow. Here again, Bennett had a story that reveals much about Gurdjieff. Many years later, in 1948,

Bennett went to see Gurdjieff in Paris. Bennett lost his own mother, and Gurdjieff asked him about her. Then Gurdjieff made the curious comment: 'She is in need of help because she cannot find her way by herself. My own mother is already free and I can help her. Through her your mother can be helped, but you have to bring them into contact.' He instructed Bennett to take two chairs, and to stand in front of them, envisaging his own mother in one and Gurdjieff's mother in the other. Bennett tried hard for weeks, and found the exercise immensely difficult. On one occasion he sobbed for half an hour. Nothing seemed to be happening, until one day he became aware of presences in the room. These finally took the shape of his own mother and Gurdjieff's. Eventually, he felt that the two had established contact, and experienced an immense wave of relief and gratitude. Gurdjieff had told him: 'You cannot help her yourself: but through my mother I can help you.' It seems clear that Gurdjieff believed that he was somehow in contact with his mother after death.

The motor accident involved another tragedy. For some time Gurdjieff's wife had been suffering from cancer, and he had been making immense efforts to cure her by a technique from Central Asia that made use of astral power. His motor accident made this impossible; his wife died soon after. Yet a story told by Olga de Hartmann again demonstrates his curious powers. Towards the end, his wife was in such pain that she could not eat, or even drink. Gurdjieff asked for half a glass of water, and held it in his hands for five minutes; then he asked Olga de Hartmann to give it to her. His wife succeeded in drinking the water without pain, and was suddenly able to take liquid food again.*

Slowly, Gurdjieff recovered from the effects of his accident. He was inclined to believe that some 'hostile power' had caused it, and was trying actively to interfere with his work. But he now directed all his energies to writing. Much of his income now came from America, where Orage had started his own Gurdjieff group. Gurdjieff was not entirely happy about Orage as a teacher of his ideas, but he was grateful for the money.

*This technique – of transmitting healing power through water – is well known to 'spirit healers', and in recent years, experiments have suggested that an actual change takes place in the molecular structure of the water.

Gurdjieff's writing – particularly *Beelzebub* – will always be a matter of contention. The style is so impossibly involved that it makes an immediate impression of pretentious nonsense. It is also full of outlandish words: kundabuffer, gaidoropoolo, geneotriamazikamnian, harhrinhrarh, blastegoklornian, and dozens of others. (The last means simply the circumference of the atmosphere of our planet, which leads one to wonder why Gurdjieff needed to invent this new word.) The explanation offered by many of his followers is that the style has been made deliberately difficult in order to force the reader to work at it. This view is reinforced by the study of his early book *Herald of Coming Good*, where the difficulty of the style is due simply to the insertion of dozens of subordinate clauses. Here is an example:

> This protracted and, for me, absolutely unnatural life, absolutely irreconcilable, too, in every way with the traits that had entrenched themselves in my individuality by the time of my maturity, was the direct consequence of my decision, founded upon the results of my previous study of a whole series of historic precedents with a view, first of all, – to preventing, by to a certain degree unnatural outward manifestations of myself, the formation, in relation to me, that already noted from ancient times 'something', termed by the great Solomon, King of Juda, 'Tzvarnoharno', which, as was set out by our ancestors, forms itself by a natural process in the communal life of people as an outcome of a conjunction of the evil actions of the so-called 'common people' and leads to the destruction of both him that tries to achieve something for general human welfare and of all that he has accomplished to this end.

Here, Bennett's explanation that 'Tzvarnoharno' is probably derived from the Pahlavi word for majesty does nothing to make Gurdjieff's meaning any clearer. Fortunately, a passage in his last book, *Life Is Real Only Then, When 'I Am'* throws some light on it; Gurdjieff says there that he considers his serious motor accident a manifestation of that 'something' accumulating in the common life of people, which seems to imply that it is a kind of hostility directed – unconsciously – at those who have achieved too much success.

In any case, it is clear that the obscurity of the passage is increased by Gurdjieff's habit of inserting a dozen parentheses into the sentence. This, I suspect, is a habit of mind rather than a deliberate attempt to irritate the reader. Gurdjieff's spoken lectures were always clear and to the point. But when he took up a pen, his mind flowed naturally into a more elaborate and flowery eastern mould.

Orage was of the opinion that when it came to expressing his ideas on paper, Gurdjieff was simply incompetent. William Seabrook came to hold the same opinion. He tells how, in January 1931, Gurdjieff asked him to invite a group of cultured New Yorkers to Gurdjieff's apartment to hear a reading from his new book. Marvellous and elaborate eastern food had been prepared (Gurdjieff was a celebrated cook). The audience included the writer Lincoln Steffens and the psychologist J. B. Watson. After the reading had been going on for some time, Watson interrupted, saying that this was either an elaborate joke, or it was piffle. In either event, it might be better to drop the reading and talk. The author accepted this without offence, and was so amusing and witty during the meal that the guests began to press him to admit that his book was a joke. Gurdjieff, according to Seabrook, remained unoffended, but implied that it was simply above their heads.

Whatever else *Beelzebub* is, it is certainly not a joke. Gurdjieff himself makes this clear. He writes that in 1927, after three years of hard work, he realized that he had not, after all, succeeded in conveying his ideas to his readers, and that extensive rewriting would be necessary. His exhaustion and the difficulties of authorship made him contemplate suicide. But the book *was* totally rewritten. There can be no doubt that, even after these immense labours, it is still not a book for those approaching Gurdjieff for the first time. (I know one highly intelligent man who has remained unalterably convinced that Gurdjieff is a charlatan because he attempted to become acquainted with his ideas through *Beelzebub*.) On the other hand Bennett, who was thoroughly acquainted with Gurdjieff's main ideas, told me that he had read it a dozen times, and that each time he had found new meanings that he had never noticed before. On the whole, it is probably safe to assume that it is the most important single product of Gurdjieff's immensely productive life.

The tremendous labours involved in writing *Beelzebub* brought Gurdjieff another important insight. He tells how he was sitting on the bench at the Prieuré where he used to sit with his wife and mother, and that it suddenly struck him that his creativity had been increased by the suffering he had experienced as a result of their deaths. In effect, this suffering had strengthened his 'essence'. He had also noted, when lying in bed after his accident, that friends who came to visit him sucked away his energy, leaving him exhausted. They were sucking away what he called *hanblezoin*, or the energy of the astral body, which is essential to creative work. The insight that came to Gurdjieff was that *hanblezoin* must be created by conscious effort and by 'intentional suffering' – the kind of suffering that saints experience on their bed of nails.

With this in mind, Gurdjieff began deliberately ridding himself of many disciples – like the Hartmanns. He felt that not only were they building up too much dependence on him, but that they were making him too comfortable. A quarrel about some English kippers was used as a pretext for sending the Hartmanns to live in Paris in 1929. Various other disciples were also requested to leave. Yet all who left remained loyal to Gurdjieff, convinced that this was not mere caprice.

Orage had to bear an unusually difficult rejection. Gurdjieff came to New York while he was in England, and required Orage's group to sign a document agreeing to break off relations with Orage. When Orage was shown this document, he took the blow calmly, and signed it himself.

In trying to assess Gurdjieff's motives for actions like this, it is as well to bear in mind a story told by Olga de Hartmann. Gurdjieff suggested that she should ask her parents to leave Leningrad and come to the Prieuré, since political conditions were becoming increasingly dangerous. Her sister and parents came, but were not happy at Fontainebleau 'because,' as Mme de Hartmann says, 'of the ruthless manner in which Mr Gurdjieff very often spoke with all of us.' One morning, Gurdjieff and Olga's father were sitting on a bench when she came to ask some question. Gurdjieff answered her angrily, and her father looked upset and miserable. Then Gurdjieff turned to her father and said: 'You see, father, what you make me do. You never shouted at your daughter, so she has not had this experience, and all sorts of impressions are necessary for people. So now I am obliged to do it in your place.' Her father, apparently, understood what he meant.

'*And all sorts of impressions are necessary for people.*' This seems to have been the principle behind some of Gurdjieff's most puzzling actions. Peters himself came to recognize this after a particularly traumatic experience. In 1934, Peters had to go to Chicago, and Gurdjieff announced that he would accompany him. The trip was a nightmare. Gurdjieff arrived late at the railway station, and made Peters go and make up a story to have the train delayed. Peters actually succeeded in doing this. It took three-quarters of an hour to get Gurdjieff to his berth, complaining loudly all the way, although the conductor kept begging him to be silent for the sake of the sleeping passengers. Gurdjieff then decided to eat, drink and smoke, until the conductor threatened to throw him off at the next stop. When Peters lost his temper, Gurdjieff asked him sadly why he was treating him in this way.

Once in his berth, Gurdjieff demanded water – to the fury of the other passengers. He settled down to sleep only at 4 a.m. The next morning, at breakfast, Gurdjieff made an endless fuss about wanting yogurt, then, after driving everybody to a frenzy, ate a normal American breakfast. During the remainder of the trip he kept his fellow passengers in a constant state of annoyance by smoking, drinking heavily, and producing strong smelling cheeses.

When they reached Chicago, Peters told him angrily that he was leaving, and Gurdjieff set up such an outcry that Peters had to consent to going with him and the group of adoring disciples. Peters finally shocked the disciples by denouncing Gurdjieff in four letter words, and strode out. But when he saw Gurdjieff again in New York a few years later, it struck him that the whole incident had been designed to force him out of his attitude of blind hero-worship. It had undoubtedly worked.

Peters has another story that illustrates Gurdjieff's skill in 'handling' people, as well as his sense of humour. Gurdjieff had invited a group of 'important' people to dinner. Before they arrived, he asked Peters to teach him every obscene word and phrase he knew. The guests arrived – many of them journalists – and sat down to dinner. In a slightly patronizing manner, they began asking Gurdjieff questions about his work. Gurdjieff then began to explain that most people are not really motivated by the desire for truth or order, but by their sexual drives. He spoke to a well-dressed, attractive woman, and told her that the care she took of her appearance was based on a 'desire to fuck'. He began to speak of his own sexual prowess, then of the sexual habits of various races, always using the crudest words he could find. After the meal, the guests began to flirt with one another, and many of them were soon lying around in a state of partial undress. The woman whom Gurdjieff had complimented began making passes at him, while another woman tried to corner Peters in the kitchen; when he rebuffed her, she accused him of being 'that dirty old man's little faggot'.

Suddenly, in a stentorian voice, Gurdjieff called them to attention, and began to mock them, telling them that they now knew what kind of people they really were. He ended by saying that he deserved to be paid for giving them this lesson, and would be glad to accept cheques. As a result, he collected several thousand dollars.

By 1935, Gurdjieff had also given up writing, abandoning a final book, *Life is Real Only Then, When 'I Am'*, when it was less than half finished. Since he was still scarcely more than sixty (or only fifty-eight, if the date of his passport is accurate), it seems unlikely that he regarded his life-work as finished. But the Institute had collapsed, and he seemed to have no plans for further writing. The Prieuré was sold in 1933, and when Peters met Gurdjieff in New York in the mid-thirties he was again short of money, which he earned by treating drug-addicts and alcoholics. (This period, fortunately, was brief.) So Gurdjieff continued to lecture and teach in America – dividing his time between the groups in Chicago and New York – while Ouspensky carried on the work in London.

Both were in the paradoxical position of wanting to spread the teaching, yet wanting to prevent it from spreading too fast or indiscriminately. Peters comments of the Chicago group:

> They seemed to me to have been attracted to his teaching for a variety of not very good reasons – because of loneliness, or perhaps because they considered themselves misfits or outcasts. Most of them had dabbled in the arts, theosophy, the occult . . . I began to sense a certain danger in his teaching when it was carried on without his personal supervision.

Ouspensky's London pupils were made to behave like conspirators, and ordered not to discuss the teaching with any outsiders; when Bennett asked permission to quote Ouspensky, he was refused.

The chief difference between Gurdjieff and Ouspensky, as teachers, was that Gurdjieff always seems to have found human beings amusing and interesting, while Ouspensky struck his followers as a scientist, a man wholly preoccupied with spreading the idea of the 'fight against sleep', with little interest in people as individuals. Gurdjieff seems to have derived a great deal of quiet amusement from his disciples. Peters tells a story about a girl, a dancer, who achieved a certain amount of authority within one of his groups, but was aggressive and difficult. One day, after she had openly challenged some statement he had made during a lecture, Gurdjieff sent her a message asking her to come to his room alone at three in the morning, where he would show her some astonishing things. Peters relayed the message, and the girl was indignant; she said she recognized a proposition when she heard it, and would never have anything more to do with Gurdjieff. When Peters carried back this message, Gurdjieff chuckled with satisfaction and said this is precisely what he had hoped. He added the interesting remark that it was just as well that she had turned him down, because he would not have had time to deal with the 'reverberations' that would have followed if she had accepted his invitation. The implication seems to be that no 'involvement' can be without consequences. 'Casual sex' is a contradiction in terms. Again, one senses that Gurdjieff was aware of certain underlying laws of human existence.

Shortly before the Second World War, Gurdjieff returned to Paris. When the Germans invaded France, he seems to have ignored pleas to escape to 'free France', but stayed on at his flat in the Rue des Colonels Rénards. One of the first of the American followers to see him after the war was Fritz Peters who – as we have seen in the first chapter – came to him suffering from deep nervous depression, which Gurdjieff cured instantaneously with some kind of infusion of vital energy. He told Peters that he had managed to live comfortably during the war by selling rugs; he also owned a company that made false eyelashes. He also told Peters that he had made deals with many people – Germans, policemen, black marketeers – and so had managed to keep himself supplied with necessities like tobacco and brandy. He was still surrounded by disciples, who also provided part of his income. But Peters also noticed a number of rather shabby, old people who visited the flat, and whom Gurdjieff treated with a kindliness and gentleness that was completely unlike his attitude to his students; he apparently regarded these as his 'pensioners'.

Other American students began to drift back to Paris. Bennett came with his wife, who was suffering from a mysterious illness. He found Gurdjieff looking older and sadder, although he held himself as erect as ever. Gurdjieff was now casually dressed in open necked shirt, untidy trousers and a red fez. During lunch – at which about forty people were wedged into the tiny dining room – he noticed that Mrs Bennett was in pain. Gurdjieff fetched two pills and told her to swallow them. Later he asked her: 'Where is your pain now?' She answered: 'It is gone.' 'I ask you where *is* it now?' Her eyes filled with tears and she answered: 'You have taken it.' In fact, her health now suddenly improved.

Kenneth Walker and his wife also came to the flat; Walker had been a student of Ouspensky's for many years, having been introduced to him by Maurice Nicoll, one of the original Prieuré group. Walker describes the flat as looking like a crowded junk shop. Gurdjieff entered while they were all listening to a reading from *Beelzebub*. Walker comments that he was shorter and stouter than he expected; he also noted the piercing eyes. Again, an enormous number of people were present at lunch, and everyone was made to drink toasts in Armagnac or vodka. Gurdjieff explained once that he always made his guests half drunk because this was the quickest way of making them drop the 'personality' and reveal what was inside them. It was after this encounter that Walker's wife described Gurdjieff as a magician.

Several other Ouspensky disciples visited the flat. Walker remarks that 'too much theorizing [had tended] to make the minds of his London followers too rigid, and our behaviour too calculated and grim. We were in danger of acquiring the chapel-going faces of Plymouth Brethren.' Gurdjieff's boozy lunches and dinners (which always began well after midnight) were just what was needed to make them relax and bring them closer together. This again illustrates the basic difference between Gurdjieff and Ouspensky. Walker observes that Gurdjieff gave him a completely new attitude towards the 'work'. Ouspensky was a disciplinarian; when he set a task, Walker carried it out as scrupulously as possible, but never tried to go further than that.

With Gurdjieff I began to develop a sense of personal responsibility and to experience a new freedom. At the same time it was a freedom which must be very carefully used for the punishment for error was very great. It was the punishment of seeing one's teacher gravely inconvenienced by one's mistake, and it was difficult to be in close touch with Gurdjieff for long without developing an affection for him.

That autumn – 1948 – Gurdjieff went back to America once more. Ouspensky, convinced that Europe was doomed, had carried on his work in New York during the war years, but illness finally drove him back to London. He died in 1948, leaving the manuscript of his most important book, *Fragments of an Unknown Teaching*, later published under the title *In Search of the Miraculous*. Gurdjieff took over the Ouspensky group in New York, and his impact is described by Irmis B. Popoff in her book *Gurdjieff*. She speaks of the enormous impression of kindness and compassion that he made.

Gurdjieff's stay in New York seems to have been as hectic as his days in Paris – vast meals for dozens of people, dancing classes, lectures, interminable sessions in Child's Restaurant. Gurdjieff also read the manuscript of Ouspensky's book, and prepared his own *Beelzebub* for publication; he admired Ouspensky's work, but insisted that *Beelzebub* was a better source book of his teaching.

Child's Restaurant was the scene of one of his last displays of 'magical' power. Bennett was in New York, and went to join Gurdjieff in Child's one morning. Gurdjieff told him to take a sheet of paper and write. Bennet found his hand writing automatically, in a style that was not his own. It was an announcement of the forthcoming publication of *Beelzebub*, and a request that as many pupils as possible should buy copies at £100 per copy. Later that day, Gurdjieff read the letter aloud to a gathering of pupils, many of whom commented that no one but Gurdjieff could have written it.

Gurdjieff returned to Paris the following spring. Kenneth Walker noticed that his health was deteriorating seriously, and advised him to have an operation to remove fluid from his abdomen. Gurdjieff apparently ignored this advice.

Bennett also continued to see him regularly, and found that Gurdjieff was as demanding as ever. Bennett stretched himself to breaking point to meet impossible requests, until it suddenly dawned on him that this was another of Gurdjieff's 'tricks'. Bennett's problem was an inability to say no, and Gurdjieff was trying to teach him to develop it. When this realization came to him, he experienced immense relief.

Once again, with Gurdjieff's help, Bennett began having unusual experiences. When reading aloud before the evening meal at Gurdjieff's flat, he suddenly left his body and stood several feet away, listening to his voice continuing to read. After that, he experienced a return of the ability to command his emotional states at will; he also discovered that he could be aware of events happening in other places. One day, to confirm this, he rang his wife in London, and verified that she had been at a certain meeting with women friends, as he had seen during his state of 'clairvoyance'.

In October, when Bennett returned to Paris, it was clear that Gurdjieff was now very ill. Eighteen months before, he had been involved in another car accident that had caused serious damage; Bennett had then been impressed by the vitality that prevented him from dying. Now, with his legs swollen with dropsy, he seemed to have no more will to live. Bennett found him sitting in a café on the morning of Saturday, 22 October 1949, looking ill and tired. He told Bennett: 'The next five years will decide. It is the beginning of a new world. Either the old world will make me "Tchik" (making a sound like a louse being squashed) or I will make (i.e. squash) the old world "Tchik". Then the new world can begin.' Which suggests that Gurdjieff expected to live for at least another five years. Bennett drove home with him in his car, an act of considerable courage, for Gurdjieff was always an atrocious driver, and now his legs were so swollen that he was unable to use the brake. Crossing the Avenue Carnot, a lorry swept down towards them; Gurdjieff continued at the same pace, missing it by a hair's breadth. In order to stop the car outside his flat, he had to allow it to run down.

Four days later, Gurdjieff's American doctor saw him, and ordered him to be moved to the American hospital. His blood pressure was too high to inject serum. The enormous quantity of liquid was drained off from his stomach, but it was apparently too late. By the following Saturday, 29 October, he was dead. There seemed to be some doubt even about that. Four hours after his death, his forehead was still warm. And when Bennett stood alone beside the body in the chapel of the American Hospital, he could hear someone breathing –

even when he held his breath and closed his eyes. He suspected Gurdjieff of a last practical joke.

When the autopsy was performed, the doctors were baffled. His intestines were in such a state of disintegration and decay that he should have been dead years ago.

Eight

Gurdjieff versus Ouspensky?

BEELZEBUB'S *Tales to his Grandson*, which Gurdjieff regarded as the essence of his teaching, is over twelve hundred pages long. Ouspensky's *In Search of the Miraculous*, undoubtedly the best summary of Gurdjieff's ideas, is over four hundred. Even for the intelligent and well-disposed reader, this represents a considerable problem. According to Gurdjieff and Ouspensky, it is an inescapable problem. The length demands from the reader a certain effort which is indispensable if the ideas are to be grasped and digested, rather than merely swallowed whole.

Yet Ouspensky's own book amounts to a compromise with his original position, that the ideas could only be conveyed directly, from teacher to pupil, and that any attempt to convey them in writing would dilute their very essence, and so falsify them.

What bothered Ouspensky was the modern tendency to simplify important ideas for popular consumption: *Relativity Made Easy, Kant for Beginners*. But he was overlooking a vital point: that such books are not necessarily for the lazy. If you intend to try to learn about Kant or relativity from scratch, you would undoubtedly do better to start with a simplified account rather than trying to plunge directly into *The Critique of Pure Reason* or Einstein's collected mathematical papers.

With this in mind, then, let us see whether it is possible to make the approach to Gurdjieff less formidable.

We might well begin with the conflict between Gurdjieff and Ouspensky. Bennett writes: 'Gurdjieff frequently complained that Ouspensky had ruined his pupils by his excessively intellectual approach, and that he [Gurdjieff] did better with people who came to him with no preparation at all.' And we have already noted Kenneth Walker's observation that Ouspensky had made them too rigid and grim. Bennett quotes Ouspensky as telling his pupils that 'all in London should make sure to avoid the smallest departure from the letter of the System as contained in the writings I have left.' When Bennett sent Ouspensky a paper he had written on the fifth dimension, Ouspensky dismissed it with the remark: 'Nothing new can be found by intellectual processes alone. There is only one hope: that we should find the way to work with the higher emotional centre.' And he added the sad comment: 'And we do not know how this is to be done.'

In short, Ouspensky's basic approach is curiously pessimistic and negative. He believes that the 'System' is man's only salvation from his 'mechanicalness', from his complete inability to 'do'. But he feels that the road is tremendously steep and difficult. Bennett's wife told him: 'You do not trust yourself, and that is not good . . . Why don't you follow your own line more, and stop trying to imitate Mr Ouspensky?' She recognized that this was the trouble – Ouspensky's gloomy, almost Calvinistic attitude to the 'System'.

Gurdjieff's approach was altogether more optimistic. He told his Prieuré students: 'Every man can achieve this independent mind: everyone who has a serious wish can do it.' There is no suggestion here that the path is too difficult for all but the most desperate or determined; a serious wish was enough – the kind of seriousness you would have to bring to learning a foreign language or studying mathematics.

Yet from descriptions of life at the Prieuré, it seems clear that Gurdjieff himself was at least partly responsible for Ouspensky's attitude. The immense physical efforts required of the disciples, the fasts, the rebukes and emotional shocks, all seem to imply that freedom from 'mechanicalness' demands an almost superhuman dedication. And Bennett himself had his doubts. He writes: 'But in spite of these results there was something not right. It was too frenzied, we were all in too much of a hurry . . . We all wanted to run before we could walk.'

And, however hesitantly, Bennett blames Gurdjieff:

> Looking back, it seems Gurdjieff was still experimenting. He wanted to see what European people were capable of. He discovered that we were prepared to make efforts that few Asiatic people will accept – for the simple reason that on the whole Asiatic people are not in a hurry. The difference is deceptive and it may be that Gurdjieff misjudged the capacity for effort, and took it for ability to accept the need for inward change. As I see it now, we did not really grasp the profound change of attitude towards oneself that is needed before the process of the 'Work' can act freely in us. We were perhaps misled by Gurdjieff's insistence on effort and yet more effort.

Now, as all the major religious teachers have recognized, excessive effort can in itself be counter-productive. For the 'I' that makes the effort is the anxiety-ridden left-brain ego. This conscious 'will' is hampered by its own self-awareness. The 'true will' seems to operate from elsewhere – from the realm of 'essence' – which, as Gurdjieff says, is located elsewhere in the brain. And it is actually repressed and rendered non-operative by the fussy anxiety of the left-brain 'personality'.

If this is, in fact, a valid criticism – not only of Ouspensky's approach but of Gurdjieff's – then it suggests that the 'System' was not as complete or final as Ouspensky liked to believe. No one had any doubt that it *worked*. Leading followers like Ouspensky, Bennett, Orage, de Hartmann, Walker, have left us in no doubt about that. Yet it seems equally clear that all of them ended with a certain sense of unfulfilment, as if they had somehow failed to gain what had originally been promised. Accounts of Ouspensky's last years make it clear that he was a tired and sad man. Bennett was struck by Gurdjieff's sadness when he saw him after twenty-five years, and this sadness can be seen in all the later photographs.

It may seem naïve to expect that the 'Work' should bring about the same kind of inner transformation – complete with visions and ecstasies – of religious conversion. Yet it *does* seem reasonable to expect it to bring about some degree of inner satisfaction and serenity. And accounts by various Gurdjieff disciples make it clear that it failed even in this respect. The problem of why this should be so presents an interesting challenge. At all events, it is worth examining more closely.

Perhaps the best way of beginning is to try to re-define the question which Gurdjieff's 'System' attempts to solve.

Everyday consciousness is limited by 'mechanicalness', 'the robot'. We become so accustomed to the repetitive routine of everyday life that we end by being bound hand and foot by habit, like a fly wrapped in spider-web. Yet no one, even the laziest, is really happy with this state of affairs, for we recognize that it robs us of a certain intensity, a feeling of being fully alive. We need security; but it tends to conflict with that desire to be 'wide awake'. *This* is more often associated with insecurity. Sartre, for example, remarked that he had never felt so alive as when he was in the French Resistance, and was likely to be arrested and shot at any moment.

This conflict produces the problem that I have identified as 'the dilemma of the Outsider'. Dominant human beings prefer insecurity and intensity to security and boredom. Of course, even the less dominant ones hanker after 'intensity'; but they are unwilling to trade it for security. The ideal state of affairs for everyone would be a combination of security *and* intensity. This has, in fact, been the basic aim of all the major religions. For example, a monastery is a place whose walls guarantee security, but whose inhabitants are dedicated to spiritual intensity through discipline and prayer. Throughout history, prophets, saints and spiritual teachers have addressed themselves to this problem: to prescribe a mode of life that combines 'wide awakeness' with a reasonable degree of security and normality.

Extreme solutions have never been popular. The Buddha turned his back on the harsher forms of yogic discipline. The Fathers of the Church have always frowned on 'enthusiasm' (i.e. fanaticism) and have burnt some of its more notorious advocates. The trouble is that the less extreme solutions – those that made room for human timidity and laziness – have always been just as unsatisfactory in the long run. Man seems to be driven by a deep-rooted craving to escape his normal limitations.

Gurdjieff's method is remarkable for the scientific precision of its approach to the problem of mechanicalness. We need security in order to realize our creative potentialities, since a man without security can think of nothing but where his next meal is coming from. But security causes a certain *automatic* relaxation, precisely analogous to the way that a hypnotist can send a good trance subject to sleep with a snap of his fingers. Recent experiments with sensory deprivation – in the 'black room' – have demonstrated this even more clearly. Deprived of all external stimuli, the mind not only falls asleep; it literally disintegrates. We are held together by external challenges and problems. Deprived of these, we drift apart, like a raft whose ropes have been cut.

Theoretically, the answer is simple enough. We must de-hypnotize ourselves, devise ropes that will continue to hold even when we have achieved security; *inner* bonds that will hold even when the external bonds have dissolved. Gurdjieff decided that the answer lay in what might be called 'artificial insecurity' – not hair shirts and beds of nails, but intellectual efforts, physical disciplines, emotional shocks. It was a combination of the way of the fakir, the monk and the yogi – physical, intellectual and emotional effort. But Gurdjieff also recognized the need for a 'fourth way', which he called the way of the 'cunning man'. This is the man who has a certain precise knowledge, and who uses this 'inside information' to gain his end. That is to say, Gurdjieff was aware that mere brute force and effort are *not* the whole answer. In spite of which, the emphasis in the 'System' swung inevitably towards 'effort and yet more effort'.

In the case of Ouspensky, it is easy to see what went wrong. His starting point was his insistence on man's mechanicalness, his total inability to act or 'to do'. In fact, man's mechanicalness – or bondage – is *not* the starting point, either of Gurdjieff's System or any other. If we were mechanical all the time, we would feel no need to search for 'freedom'. The real starting point is the *glimpse of freedom* – the moments of intensity, of 'wide-awakeness' – what Abraham Maslow calls 'the peak experience'. *These* are what make us dissatisfied with our ordinary states of consciousness.

The next thing we note is that we experience glimpses of freedom every time some problem or emergency *galvanizes us to a sense of urgency*. This became the centre of gravity of Gurdjieff's method: to train his pupils to a permanent sense of urgency. Beelzebub tells his grandson that the only way mankind can be saved is by developing an 'organ' which would enable us to grasp the inevitability of our own death, and of the death of everyone around us. The point is underlined in the fragment of a lost story (described by Bennett) about a man who wakes up after dying 'and realizes that he had lost the chief instrument of his life, his body, and recalls all he could have done with it while he was still alive.'

One way of creating this sense of emergency is to seek out challenge. Graham Greene has described how, as a bored teenager, he played Russian roulette with a loaded revolver; when the hammer clicked on an empty chamber, 'it was as if a light had been turned on . . . and I felt that life contained an infinite number of possibilities.' Greene had chosen a rather dangerous way of 'shaking the mind awake', but his experience makes us clearly aware that the mind (or the brain) contains a *mechanism* for getting rid of the robot and waking us up. It can be switched on, like a light.

A little 'self-observation' makes us aware that this 'mechanism' could also be compared to a powerful coiled spring inside the brain. When we are galvanized by a sense of emergency or excitement, some deep source of will inside us *winds* the spring up tight, and we experience a sense of power and control.

Unfortunately, this 'spring' is only partly within our conscious control – the control of the 'personality'. It lies in the realm of that 'other self' – what Gurdjieff calls essence. The 'personality' *lacks authority* to convince this 'other self' of its seriousness. The spring responds to what might be called 'the vibration of seriousness'. This is why a hypnotist – the voice of outside authority – can persuade it to make efforts that are far beyond the power of the conscious will. Significantly, Gurdjieff understood the nature of hypnosis – a problem that still baffles modern psychology; he defines it as the suspension of 'false consciousness', the 'ruling master of their common presence', so that 'genuine consciousness' can make itself felt.* That is to say, it is the suspension of 'left-brain consciousness' (which, as Gurdjieff recognized, is the ruling ego of our double-consciousness), so that the far more powerful right-brain consciousness can express itself without interference.

This left-brain consciousness is both man's greatest triumph and his undoing. With its logical precision it has enabled him

---

*'An omission from p 568 of *Beelzebub*' – Guide and Index to *All and Everything*, p 673.

to create civilization, as well as the immense body of modern scientific knowledge. But in order to operate at full efficiency, it requires the backing of man's 'other' being – instinctive or intuitive consciousness. This explains why we feel most 'alive' when we are engaged in some important activity, something that gives us a sense of crisis or emergency. Then that 'other self' gives left-brain consciousness its full backing and support. But if I watch television for too long, or try to read a long book in a single sitting, I begin to experience an odd sense of unreality. I feel 'lightweight', unreal. This is because our 'other self' has decided that no backing is required; we are dealing with unrealities, so it feels it can go off duty.

This, then, defines our problem. In this world of trivial emergencies and unimportant decisions, man has developed a reliance on left-brain consciousness that dominates his existence. He has become so accustomed to this 'lightweight' consciousness, with its accompanying sense of unreality, that he has almost forgotten what 'real consciousness' is like. His 'other self' is almost permanently off-duty.

How can it be persuaded to return to its proper work of 'backing' left-brain consciousness? Many methods have been suggested. D. H. Lawrence thought sex was the answer. Hemingway advocated 'adventure' – big game hunting, bullfighting, and so on. But Gurdjieff saw that these are insufficient. That 'other self' has to be galvanized and shaken awake again and again, day after day. The 'personality' (left-brain consciousness) has to be undermined by crisis and unexpected challenges. Knowledge is also important, of course – understanding of the mechanisms of the 'computer'. But theoretical knowledge once again strengthens the rational ego – what Lawrence called 'head consciousness'. So the correct solution is a balanced diet – theoretical knowledge carefully mixed with 'effort'. This was Gurdjieff's solution, and it was transformed into a rigid system by Ouspensky.

Gurdjieff himself perceived the dangers of rigidity. He recognized that in matters as difficult and complicated as this – the attempt to understand the mystery of man's inner-being – language can easily betray us. It is necessary to keep an open mind, and approach the problem from many different angles. The result is that anyone who reads Gurdjieff's three books, then turns to accounts of his lectures by disciples, will often find himself puzzled by contradictions. These contradictions are a proof that Gurdjieff was not the recipient of some mysterious 'ancient wisdom', which he passed on to his followers like the tables of the law. He was a psychologist of genius, whose insight was continually developing. His basic recognition was that man is a vast computer, with many levels of control. At present, he has so little control of this vast machine that he is virtually its slave. But theoretically, he could achieve *total* control. And since the resources of the computer seem greater than anyone has ever imagined, he could, in theory, become a kind of god.

His basic task therefore, is, to *know the computer*. This is not too difficult – in theory, at least. It merely requires constant self-observation. But the second task is far more difficult. Self-observation is best carried out in states of insight and intensity, states when the 'two consciousnesses' are in harmony and in close co-operation. *How can we induce these states at will?* If there was some simple method, man's problems would be at an end. If, for example, he could achieve it through sex, or bullfighting, or by swallowing some drug, then he would have solved the major problem of his evolution. Unfortunately, to judge by their advocates, none of these methods can give long-term satisfaction.

And what of Gurdjieff's 'System'? This can certainly show far more spectacular results. Yet, as we have seen, it could also involve his pupils in a great deal of misery, exhaustion and confusion. And for many of them, the end result was not as satisfying as they might have wished. Bennett, for example, later became a disciple of the Indonesian 'messiah' Pakh Subuh, and after that a Roman Catholic – a fairly clear indication that the 'system' left certain aspects of his nature unfulfilled.

So far in this book, I have deliberately kept my own views and attitudes in the background; but at this point it becomes necessary to admit that, after nearly three decades of absorbing Gurdjieff's ideas, I feel that there *were* a number of small but important points which that master of self-observation failed to take into account.

Gurdjieff's enormous emphasis on man's 'mechanicalness', and the difficulties of escaping it even for a moment, seems to imply that moments of 'non-mechanicalness' are rare or non-existent. In fact, as I have pointed out, this is untrue. Human beings are always experiencing flashes of 'awakeness', glimpses of freedom. T. E. Lawrence describes one of them in *Seven Pillars of Wisdom*:

> We started on one of those clear dawns that wake up the senses with the sun, while the intellect, tired after the thinking of the night, was yet abed. For an hour or two, on such a morning, the sounds, scents and colours of the world struck man individually and directly, not filtered through or made typical by thought; they seemed to exist sufficiently by themselves.

In effect, the left-brain (the 'intellect') was still asleep; so Lawrence was in a state analogous to hypnosis, in which the right-brain could perceive things directly, unimpeded by his 'thought riddled nature'. Moments like this are not rare; children experience them all the time, as Wordsworth pointed out; and even after the 'shades of the prison house' have begun to close, healthy people still experience them with reasonable frequency as moments of 'optimistic expectancy', 'peak experiences'.

The most interesting thing about these 'glimpses' is what might be called their 'meaning content'. Greene says that when his revolver failed to explode 'it was as if a light had been turned on . . . and I felt that life contains an infinite number of possibilities.' And this is common to all such experiences. They produce a sense of *revelation*, of 'absurd good news', a feeling that the world is infinitely more meaningful than we normally give it credit for. The reason is clear. We normally 'see' the world through the dark-glasses of the rational ego. (The 'I' inside my head lives in the left-brain.) When we accidentally remove the dark glasses, we are startled by the vistas of forgotten meaning that burst upon us. Clearly, this precise and fussy left-brain leaves a great deal out of account. And it is because it leaves so much out of account that it is so subject to pessimism. And *this* is what is wrong with ordinary consciousness. This is why we are slaves of the robot. Ordinary consciousness involves an in-built assumption of lack of meaning. And it is the lack of meaning that triggers the sleep mechanism. (When you feel there is nothing to look forward to, you become bored and sleepy.) If we could switch on meaning at will, as Greene switched it on with his Russian roulette, the problem of 'sleep' would vanish. *Meaning* would awaken us far more effectively than any amount of violent and exhausting effort. Meaning instantly creates energy. If only we could locate the switch of the 'light' that Greene turned on by squeezing the trigger.

But in expressing the problem in this way, we are leaving an important factor out of account. Man's 'two consciousnesses' *are* interconnected. The conscious and the unconscious do not operate as separate entities; neither do the right and left halves of the brain.

It is important to understand the way that 'negativeness' operates. When I wake up in the morning, it is my rational ego that confronts the world. If 'I' see that it is raining outside, and remember that I have a dental appointment, and that my bank manager wants to talk to me about my overdraft, my 'heart sinks'. So does my *energy*. When I am happy and full of eager expectancy, a spring of energy bubbles up from my unconscious mind; meaning creates energy. Conversely, when I feel gloomy and discouraged, my energy seems to drain away. The resultant sense of fatigue deepens my sense of discouragement; and this – unless something intervenes to cheer me up – deepens my fatigue. That is to say, there is an effect of *negative feedback* between my 'two selves'.

If, on the contrary, I wake up to bright sunlight, and remember that in a few hours time I shall be setting out on holiday, my rational ego reacts with a chortle of satisfaction, and I experience the beginning of a pleasant inward glow. 'Positive feedback' has been established.

What we observe here is that although it is the 'unconscious' that controls the energy supply, its decisions are entirely governed by the *suggestions* of the 'rational ego'. If I happen to be a weak and self-pitying sort of person, most of these suggestions will be negative, and I shall feel exhausted and depressed much of the time. If I am a cheerful and rational sort of person, my unconscious will respond to positive suggestions, my sense of meaning, by keeping me well provided with energy. Moreover, this energy will have the effect of making the world *look* a happier and brighter place – making me see *more* meaning – thus confirming my optimism.

When we consider modern humanity in general, one thing stands out fairly clearly: that our basic attitude towards existence tends to be negative, tinged with distrust. This indicates that most of us have fallen into the habit of 'negative feedback'. There seems to be good reason for this: modern life is difficult and complex; humanity faces many problems. But anyone who has understood Gurdjieff's ideas will know that these 'reasons' are irrelevant. It would be equally true to say that mankind is now happier and more comfortable than it has ever been. The real issue is our *habit of negation*.

Gurdjieff taught that this habit is stupid and unnecessary. The really important thing about man is that he possesses a possibility of real freedom, once he has grasped the fact that, at the moment, his life is almost entirely mechanical. He must turn the searchlight of his reason, his analytical processes, upon all his unconscious assumptions.

And it is when we turn the searchlight upon the contrasted activities of our 'two consciousnesses' that we grasp a fundamental truth about human existence – a truth, I suspect, that Gurdjieff only partly understood. The rational ego tends to be pessimistic because it sees things *too close up*. This is like trying to decide on the merits of a large picture by examining the canvas through a magnifying glass or microscope. In fact, such an examination, no matter how conscientious, would fail to reveal what the painter had put into the picture. Right-brain consciousness, on the other hand, deals in terms of meanings, of overall patterns. And, as we have seen, undiluted right-brain consciousness always produces the feeling of sheer delight, of 'absurd good news'.

In short, the 'worm's-eye view' of the left brain is negative by nature. The 'birds-eye view' of the right-brain is positive by nature, revealing vistas of meaning and interconnectedness that are invisible to the worm.

Our practical problem, the problem we confront every day of our lives, is to decide which of the two is telling the truth. But unless we understand that one of them deals in 'immediacy perception' and the other in 'meaning perception', we have no means of weighing their testimony. To begin with, it is the left-brain that tries to do the weighing. Second, the 'moments of vision' are so much rarer than moments of boredom and discouragement that, on purely arithmetical grounds, we are inclined to believe the negative testimony. But what we need to know is that the 'rational ego', for all its logic and clarity of perception, is essentially a microscope, which can only see things piecemeal. The 'other self' may have no power of self-expression, but it has an instantaneous grasp of meanings. Once we know this, there can be no possible doubt about which testimony we accept. The left is not fundamentally a liar, but its partial-vision leads it to incorrect inferences about the world. It is in the position of the blind beggars in Ramakrishna's parable, who try to describe an elephant by the sense of touch alone.

Then there is the most convincing piece of evidence of all: that when the right and left achieve one of their infrequent moods of harmony – those strange, relaxed moments that seem to combine insight with intellectual excitement – the left is totally convinced that the right was correct all along. It now sees clearly that its pessimism was based on false interpretation of insufficient facts; there is a sense of direct revelation that can only be expressed in the words: 'Of *course!*'

Yet since the left is, by nature, limited to piecemeal perception, the problem seems insoluble – until we realize that this is a problem we solve every day of our lives. The left is, in fact, continually accepting truths that run counter to its own perceptions. Immediacy perception tells it that the sun goes round the earth and that the earth is flat; but it has no difficulty in accepting the Copernican theory. Immediacy-perception tells it that a book is a two-dimensional object; yet it takes it for granted that it has three.

What is even more to the point is that the left's perceptions tell it that a book is merely a combination of paper and black ink; yet it knows perfectly well that a book has yet another dimension – that what matters about the book is its content, its *meaning*. A child who loves reading feels an immediate lift of the heart, a kind of instinctive delight, at the sight of a book. But it is *not* instinctive; it is 'taught'. The left may be a sceptic by nature, but it is a believer by training.

All this implies that the outcome of Gurdjieff's ideas could be more important and exciting than Gurdjieff himself ever realized. He devoted his life to solving the problem of how to re-unite the 'two consciousnesses', so that essence and personality could develop in harmony. He devised all kinds of methods for shaking 'essence' into a state of wakefulness, so as to rescue the ego from its sense of absurdity and unreality. He failed to realize that we already possess a faculty for doing it spontaneously. The mind does not need to be shaken awake; it can be educated awake. All that is required is a change of attitude. The rational ego has acquired a deeply-ingrained habit of mistrust. Western man receives his 'melting moods', his 'moments of vision', with a certain scepticism, as if they were related to being drunk. Understanding of the different functions of the 'two consciousnesses' enables us to see that this mistrust is unnecessary. The 'moments of vision' were telling the truth all along. The moment we really *grasp* this – rationally and logically, as we grasp that the earth is round – we shall begin to *see* the vision of infinite possibility that Greene experienced as he played Russian roulette; but as a steadily-held insight, not a sudden glimpse.

Greene's experience underlines another point to which Gurdjieff paid insufficient attention. The brain possesses a *mechanism* for freeing us from the robot – a mechanism that I have compared to a powerful coiled spring. If I try to contract this 'spring' by an act of will, by sheer concentration, I find the effort painful and exhausting. A sudden crisis is far more effective. Yet the really important recognition is that I *can* contract it by a determined effort of will. The mental 'muscle' I use for this purpose is undeveloped. But all muscles can be developed. In fact, if I make a habit of deliberately contracting this 'muscle' of attention or concentration, my ability to make use of the 'spring' quickly begins to develop.

And at this point, it becomes possible to answer with more precision the question: how can the right-brain be persuaded to return to its proper task of 'backing' left-brain consciousness? The solution lies in the fact that right-brain consciousness moves at a far more leisurely pace than the left. The left is always in a hurry. Which explains why it reduces the world to symbols, to flat, two-dimensional surfaces. If I glance at something quickly, I take in only its surface characteristics.

If, when I am in a hurry, something suddenly arrests my attention and arouses my interest, I immediately *slow down*, just as I would slow down in a car if I passed through interesting scenery. And this mental act of slowing-down has the immediate effect of revealing fine shades of meaning that I had previously been in too much of a hurry to notice.

In fact, man invented art specifically for this purpose of slowing him down. You cannot enjoy a picture gallery or a symphony concert without 'unwinding' and giving your full attention to the pictures or music.

And what happens when I 'slow down' and become deeply absorbed in a book or piece of music? That'other dimension' of meaning begins to open up. I suddenly become aware of my own feelings, my inner-states, at the same time that I am absorbed in the book or symphony, i.e. I achieve a state of self-remembering naturally and without undue effort. And an interesting phenomenon occurs. If I think of the 'me' of an hour ago, rushing along through the crowds, tense with anxiety, I find myself looking back on him with a kind of pitying superiority. I no longer feel identified with him. My 'personal centre of gravity' has moved from the left to the right. I am now 'identifying' with this more relaxed, perceptive self.

All this is not to say that the answer lies simply in 'relaxation'. Ordinary relaxation does not have the effect of moving the 'personal centre of gravity'. What is important here is the *mental act* that causes the slowing-down. I slow down *because* I am deeply interested, because my total attention is demanded (e.g. imagine a man defusing an unexploded bomb). Moreover, the slowing-down process also involves that 'spring' that controls our energy supply. To make a deliberate and determined effort of will is to automatically slow down. And, in fact, the slowing-down process can be achieved by a deliberate effort of willed concentration.

It is immensely important to grasp that relaxation in itself is *not* the point. The point is the *motive* behind the relaxation: the recognition that our ordinary perception does not disclose the reality of the world. If you suspected that a stranger on a train was someone you knew, wearing some kind of disguise, you would stare intently, *trying to penetrate the disguise*. Here, the basis of the 'mental act' would be your suspicion that your ordinary perception is deceiving you, and the consequent desire to deepen your perception. It is an act that we instinctively perform when we experience intense pleasure: the desire to apply a brake to the usual headlong flow of consciousness.

Once this perception of 'another dimension' has been achieved, there is an instant sense of relief, and an immediate flow of vitality, a feeling of renewal. Meaning summons energy. In this state, we can recognize clearly how our 'ordinary consciousness' runs down our energies without replenishing them. The moment consciousness is connected to meaning, the revitalizing process begins.

It can be seen why Gurdjieff's emphasis on 'effort and yet more effort' was counter-productive. Which still leaves a puzzling question: how did a psychologist as penetrating as Gurdjieff come to overlook the crucial importance of the slowing-down process, the focus upon *meaning*? The answer, I think, lies in the opening chapter of *Beelzebub*,* where he speaks of the nature of man's 'two independent consciousnesses'. He goes on to identify these as 'mechanical' consciousness created by experience (i.e. the robot) and man's 'hereditary' or instinctive consciousness. (He adds that this hereditary consciousness is what we call the 'subconscious', and that it ought to be our real consciousness.) It can be seen that this rough division misses the important fact that 'mechanical' consciousness deals with 'immediacy', while the other type is concerned with overall patterns and meanings.

The misconception is deepened in the chapter in which he speaks about 'the organ Kundabuffer' – Beelzebub's explanation of how man came to be so entrapped in illusion. Gurdjieff explains that a commission of archangels became worried in case man developed 'objective reason', and so came to object to his basic purpose on this planet, to provide 'food for the moon'. They decided to avert this possibility by planting in man an organ called Kundabuffer, which would distort his perception and cause him to mistake illusion for reality. This could be regarded as Gurdjieff's own version of the legend of original sin, Newman's 'primeval catastrophe' in which the whole human race is implicated.

But, as we have seen, it is not a question of illusion – merely of the *partial perception* of the rational ego. Close-upness deprives us of meaning. In creating a legend of illusion or sin, Gurdjieff has given his philosophy a pessimistic orientation. This is emphasized by the story of the sheep and the magician, quoted by Ouspensky. † The magician was too mean to hire shepherds; so he hypnotized his sheep, suggesting to them that they were immortal, so that no harm was being done to them when they were skinned; on the contrary, they would enjoy it. They were also told that the magician was a good master who loved his flock. These suggestions kept the

*Pages 24 and 25.
† *In Search of the Miraculous*, p 219

sheep docile until they were ready for the butchers. This, added Gurdjieff, is a very good illustration of man's position. So again, the philosophy is cast into a pessimistic mould. The need to escape becomes a matter of extreme emergency, a matter for 'effort and yet more effort'.

Which brings us to an altogether more personal and delicate question. Like Gurdjieff's disciples at the Prieuré, I have also found myself puzzling about Gurdjieff's lifelong accident-proneness. Generally speaking, it is the unhappy or self-divided people who are accident-prone. It is as if a powerful sense of purpose generated an intuitive defence system. It is true that Gurdjieff was an appalling driver; yet his two most serious accidents seem to have been through no fault of his own.

The accident-proneness seems to me to be connected with his tendency to involve himself with large numbers of people. Of course, he saw this as the only logical way to convey his teaching; yet all his attempts to set up an institute ended in disaster. The war and then the revolution closed down the Russian institute. The Ataturk revolution drove him out of Turkey. The German revolution frustrated the hope of a Berlin institute. The British Home Office put an end to the hope of an institute in Hampstead. With immense difficulty, Gurdjieff acquired the Prieuré – only to see his hopes undermined by his car accident in less than two years. At last he was forced to do what he should have considered many years before – write down his ideas. The result was two extraordinary works – *Beelzebub* and *Meetings With Remarkable Men*. But he abandoned *Life Is Real Only Then, When 'I Am'* when it was less than half-completed, and went back to the exhausting drudgery of teaching his ideas direct. The reading of *Beelzebub* – described by William Seabrook – makes it clear that he hoped that his writings would make an immediate impact. Unfortunately, the total incomprehension of ordinary literate people convinced him that this was not the answer.

If, in fact, Ouspensky had published *In Search of the Miraculous* in 1930 – at the time Gurdjieff was adding the final touches to *Beelzebub* – there seems little doubt that it would have made just the impact that *Beelzebub* failed to make. But then, Ouspensky's peculiarly narrow and puritanical view of the 'Work' convinced him that writing was somehow for-bidden. In fact, the final publication of his own book, as well as that of many brilliant books by others involved in the 'Work', proved beyond all doubt that the essence of Gurdjieff's ideas can be conveyed perfectly well on the printed page. There may, as Bennett insists, be aspects of the teaching that can only be conveyed direct from teacher to student; but generally speaking, Gurdjieff's ideas gain from being read and studied.

All this, I suspect, explains why Gurdjieff struck Bennett as a sad man in his last years. His life-work had been extraordinary; he had gone out in search of 'hidden knowledge' and found it. The 'System' he brought back was, in terms of western culture, of startling originality. He would have been less than human if he had not hoped to see these ideas make maximum impact on the world of the twentieth century. This was not vanity; all thinkers experience a desire to convey their ideas: it is part of the evolutionary impulse. Yet during his lifetime, Gurdjieff remained virtually unknown to most people. In Rom Landau's *God Is My Adventure* – one of the few things published about him in his lifetime – he is merely one of a gallery, which included Rudolf Steiner, Krishnamurti, Shri Baba, Dr Frank Buchman and 'Principal' George Jeffreys. Ironically, Ouspensky is also given a chapter to himself; Gurdjieff receives a brief – and rather patronizing – mention, but there is no indication that the 'war against sleep' was Gurdjieff's idea, not Ouspensky's.

This, it seems to me, was Gurdjieff's tragedy – that he dropped the idea of spreading his ideas by writing, and returned to the only other role he knew, that of the teacher. Accounts of his students by various writers – Fritz Peters, Margaret Anderson, Irmis Popoff – make it clear that they must have tried his patience. On the whole, a 'teacher' cannot choose his pupils; he has to take what fate sends him. Inevitably, a large proportion are fools. A few students like Bennett and Ouspensky may have consoled Gurdjieff for the poor quality of so many others; but there must have been times when he felt that fate had saddled him with a particularly heavy cross. As a published writer, Gurdjieff could have sat back and waited for people to come to him; as it was, he did it the hard way. His optimism was immense, his vitality tremendous. Yet it seems that he had to console himself with large quantities of Armagnac and big black cigars. He was the kind of man one would expect to live to be ninety; instead, he died in his early seventies. At the time of his death, he must still have wondered whether his ideas would survive. Within five years, there could be no possible doubt about it. It was Gurdjieff's bad luck that he never knew how far he had succeeded.

If Gurdjieff's ideas could be summarized in a sentence, it would be that man is like a grandfather clock driven by a watch-spring. Or like an enormous water mill driven by a muddy trickle of water. The strange paradox is that in spite of the inadequacy of his driving force, an enormous and complex mechanism *already* seems to exist. Like a ladder, man consists of many levels. The problem, then, is clear: to increase the driving force. Man may be more than half mechanical; but he can choose whether to live in a blank, hypnotized state, or whether to live as though some immense unguessed meaning lay on the other side of his curtain of everyday reality, waiting to reveal itself to a sense of purpose.

Gurdjieff's 'System' is probably the greatest single-handed attempt in the history of human thought to make us aware of the potential of human consciousness. Whether he realized it or not, his life-work *had* achieved its purpose.

Select Bibliography

Books by Gurdjieff
The Herald of Coming Good. First Appeal to Contemporary Humanity,
   Paris, 1933 (reprinted by Samuel Weiser, New York, 1973).
Beelzebub's Tales to his Grandson (All and Everything, First Series).
   Routledge and Kegan Paul, 1950.
Meetings With Remarkable Men (All and Everything, Second Series).
   Routledge and Kegan Paul, 1963.
Life is Real Only Then, When 'I Am' (All and Everything, Third Series).
   Triangle Books, New York, 1975 (privately printed).

Books by Ouspensky
Tertium Organum. A Key to the Enigmas of the World. Routledge and
   Kegan Paul, 1957.
A New Model of the Universe. Routledge and Kegan Paul, 1931.
The Psychology of Man's Possible Evolution. Hedgehog Press, 1950.
In Search of the Miraculous. Fragments of an Unknown Teaching.
   Routledge and Kegan Paul, 1950.
The Fourth Way. A Record of Talks and Answers to Questions. Routledge
   and Kegan Paul, 1957.
The Strange Life of Ivan Osokin. Hermitage House, New York, 1955.
Talks With a Devil. Turnstone Press, 1972.

Books by John Bennett
The Dramatic Universe. 4 vols., Hodder and Stoughton, 1956-1966.
Gurdjieff: A Very Great Enigma. Coombe Springs Press, 1963.
Gurdjieff Today. Coombe Springs Press, 1974.
Is There 'Life' on Earth? An Introduction to Gurdjieff. Stonehill, New
   York, 1973.

Gurdjieff: Making a New World. Turnstone Press, 1973.
Witness. The Autobiography of John G. Bennett. Turnstone Press, 1974.
What Are We Living For? Hodder and Stoughton, 1949.

Books About Gurdjieff

Anon. *Guide and Index to All and Everything: Beelzebub's Tales to His Grandson*. Toronto Traditional Studies Press, 1973.

Anon. *Gurdjieff: Views From the Real World. Early Talks as Recollected by his Pupils*. Routledge and Kegan Paul, 1973.

Anderson, Margaret. *The Unknowable Gurdjieff*. Routledge and Kegan Paul, 1962.

Butkowsky-Hewitt, Anna. *With Gurdjieff in St Petersburg and Paris*. Routledge and Kegan Paul, 1978.

Hartmann, Thomas de. *Our Life with Mr Gurdjieff*. Penguin, 1972.

Hulme, Kathryn. *Undiscovered Country: In Search of Gurdjieff*. Little, Brown and Co., Boston, 1966.

Nicoll, Maurice. *Psychological Commentaries on the Teachings of Gurdjieff*. 6 vols., Vincent Stuart, 1950-56.

Nott, C. S. *Teachings of Gurdjieff. The Journal of a Pupil*. Routledge and Kegan Paul, 1961.

—— . *Journey Through This World. The Second Journal of a Pupil*. Routledge and Kegan Paul, 1969.

Pauwels, Louis. *Gurdjieff*. Samuel Weiser, New York, 1972.

Peters, Fritz. *Boyhood With Gurdjieff*. Gollancz, 1964.

—— . *Gurdjieff Remembered*. Samuel Weiser, New York, 1971.

Popoff, Irmis B. *Gurdjieff: His Work on Myself, With Others, For The Work*. The Aquarian Press, 1978.

Reyner, J. H. *The Diary of a Modern Alchemist*. Neville Spearman, 1974.

—— . *The Gurdjieff Inheritance*. Turnstone Press, 1985.

Travers, P. L. *George Ivanovitch Gurdjieff*. Traditional Studies Press, Toronto, 1973 (an amplified account of an article that appeared in *Man, Myth and Magic*).

Walker, Kenneth. *Venture With Ideas*. Jonathan Cape, 1951 (reprinted by Neville Spearman, 1971).

—— . *The Making of Man*. Routledge and Kegan Paul, 1963.

—— . *A Study of Gurdjieff's Teaching*. Jonathan Cape, 1957.

Index

C. G. JUNG: LORD OF THE UNDERWORLD

A fascinating account of Jung's ideas and their impact on twentieth-century consciousness. With characteristic fluency, Colin Wilson traces the evolution of Jung's ideas – his break away from the 'psychoanalysis' of Freud and the development of his own techniques of 'analytical psychology'. Wilson demonstrates how Jung's experience of so-called occult phenomena as well as his clinical work led him to formulate a number of key concepts including the theory of archetypes, the collective unconsciousness, synchronicity, and the use of 'active imagination' – a technique of conscious dreaming. A clear and readable introduction for the non-specialist.

RUDOLF STEINER: THE MAN AND HIS VISION

Of all the important thinkers of the twentieth century, Rudolf Steiner, 1961-1925, is perhaps the most difficult to come to grips with. No one interested in the way esoteric thought has shaped the twentieth century can ignore Steiner, but until now there has been no genuinely accessible introduction to his ideas. **Colin Wilson** here rectifies this in a book which brings Steiner to life as a person and, for the first time, explains the key principles of his complex world-view in terms the ordinary reader can understand.